THE ART OF
MIXOLOGY

THE ART OF
MIXOLOGY

CLASSIC COCKTAILS AND CURIOUS CONCOCTIONS

LOVE FOOD™

First published 2015 by Parragon Books, Ltd.

Copyright © 2021 Cottage Door Press, LLC
5005 Newport Drive, Rolling Meadows, Illinois 60008

New recipes by Kim Davies
New photography by Mike Cooper

ISBN: 978-1-64638-211-8

Printed in China

Love Food™ is an imprint of Cottage Door Press, LLC.
Parragon Books® and the Parragon® logo are registered
trademarks of Cottage Door Press, LLC.

Notes for the Reader
This book uses both metric and imperial measurements.
Follow the same units of measurement throughout; do
not mix metric and imperial. All spoon measurements
are level: teaspoons are assumed to be 5 ml, and
tablespoons are assumed to be 15 ml. One measure is
assumed to be 25 ml/¾ fl oz. Unless otherwise stated,
milk is assumed to be full fat, eggs are medium,
pepper is freshly ground black pepper and salt is
table salt. People with nut allergies should be aware
that some of the prepared ingredients used in the
recipes in this book may contain nuts.

Garnishes, decorations and serving suggestions are all
optional and not necessarily included in the recipe
ingredients or method. The times given are only an
approximate guide. Preparation times differ according
to the techniques used by different people and the
cooking times may also vary from those given. Optional
ingredients, variations or serving suggestions have not
been included in the time calculations.

Please consume alcohol responsibly.

CONTENTS

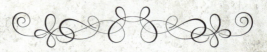

PAGE 6

INTRODUCTION

PAGE 16

GIN & VODKA

PAGE 54

RUM, WHISKIES
& BRANDY

PAGE 88

BUBBLES
(BOTH NAUGHTY & NICE)

PAGE 122

SOMETHING DIFFERENT

PAGE 156

MOCKTAILS

This beautiful book, with its delicious recipes and moreish photography, will quickly become an indispensable tool for the budding mixologist. In this comprehensive collection you'll find punches for parties, short drinks for unwinding in the evening and impressive crowd-pleasers for entertaining. All of the recipes are simply written to make them easy to follow, and even novice cocktail makers are guaranteed a winning result every time.

INTRODUCTION

Cocktails have played a colourful part in modern history and have established their place in popular culture. The history of the first cocktail remains a mystery, which has led to a number of entertaining folk tales. One of the more popular stories tells how, during the Revolutionary War, American and French soldiers frequented Betsy's Tavern to enjoy a famous alcoholic concoction of her own creation, known as 'Betsy's Bracer'. One night, amid a whirl of wild drinking and parties, one of the American soldiers stole a couple of cockerels from a neighbour's garden. He toasted his theft with his drinking companions, saying, 'Here's to the divine liquor which is as delicious to the palate as the cock's tail is beautiful to the eye'. A French officer is said to have responded to the toast with a rousing cry of 'Vive le cocktail!' - and with that, the term cocktail was born.

Since their conception, cocktail trends have come and gone - from the days of the practical cocktail (mixers were used to disguise the sometimes rough flavours of home-made spirits during the Prohibition era in America), to the fancy, frivolous cocktails favoured during the 1980s, and the pared-back, stylish cocktails made famous by stage and screen characters at the start of this century.

The art of the skilled mixologist is based on easy-to-follow principles that can set almost anyone on the right track to producing an impressive range of cocktails and mixed drinks. This book will give you all the skills you need, and you can apply these to the whole range of cocktail recipes here. Simply read up on the terminology and techniques that follow and get started on the recipes - before long you'll be mixing and shaking with the best of them.

ESSENTIAL EQUIPMENT

COCKTAIL SHAKER

The standard cocktail shaker has a capacity of 500 ml/18 fl oz. It has a double lid, which incorporates a perforated strainer. If yours does not have an integral strainer, you will need a separate one.

MIXING GLASS

This is used for making stirred cocktails. You can use any large container or jug, but you can also buy professional mixing glasses.

STRAINER

A bar or 'Hawthorn' strainer is the perfect tool to prevent ice and other ingredients being poured from the shaker or mixing glass into the serving glass. You could use a small nylon strainer instead.

BAR SPOON

This long-handled spoon is used for stirring cocktails in a mixing glass.

JIGGER OR MEASURE

This small measuring cup is often double-ended and shaped like an hourglass. Standard jiggers are 25 ml and 35 ml, while imperial jiggers are 1 fl oz and 1½ fl oz, representing 1 and 1½ measures respectively. It is the proportions of the various ingredients, not the specific quantities, that are crucial. If you don't have a jigger, you can use the small lid of your cocktail shaker or a shot glass.

MUDDLER

This miniature masher is used for crushing ingredients, such as herbs, in the base of a glass. You can also use a mortar and pestle.

OTHER EQUIPMENT

Equipment that is useful includes: a corkscrew, cocktail sticks, a citrus reamer and zester, chopping boards, knives, jugs, ice buckets and tongs, and a blender for creamy cocktails and slushes. Optional extras include swizzle sticks and straws.

MARTINI GLASS

The most immediately recognizable cocktail glass, the Martini glass has a conical shape that helps prevent the ingredients separating, while the stem keeps the drink cool.

COUPETTE GLASS

This glass is based on the earlier champagne coupe, originally used for serving bubbly. The wide bowl is perfect for rimming with salt, making it the ideal glass for serving Margaritas.

HURRICANE GLASS

The shape of this large, short-stemmed glass is said to resemble the hurricane lamp, from which it gets its name. It was originally used for the famous Hurricane cocktail at Pat O'Brien's bar in New Orleans, but today it's more usually associated with exotic frozen and blended cocktails.

CHAMPAGNE FLUTE

The tapered shape of this tall, thin glass is designed to reduce the surface area of the liquid, keeping the champagne bubbly for longer.

HIGHBALL GLASS

Highball glasses are tall and suitable for simple drinks that have a high proportion of mixer to spirit. They are versatile enough to be substituted for the similar, but slightly larger, Collins glass.

LOWBALL GLASS

The terms 'lowball', 'rocks' and 'old-fashioned' are often used to refer to short, squat tumblers. They are perfect for holding ice and are used to serve any spirit 'on the rocks'. They are also useful for short mixed drinks.

SHOT GLASS

A home-bar essential, the shot glass holds just enough liquid to be downed in a single mouthful. Shot glasses have thick bases so that they can withstand being slammed on the bar.

IRISH COFFEE GLASS

The two key features of an Irish coffee glass are heatproof glass and a handle, both of which make it suitable for hot cocktails, such as toddies.

MIXING METHODS

Creating a cocktail is not brain surgery but it does require the deft touch of a skilled mixologist. The better your mixing techniques, the better the quality of the cocktail. Mixing a cocktail is not just a matter of throwing all the ingredients together in a glass, giving them a stir and hoping for the best - there are many different mixing methods, all of which have benefits. The following are the most commonly used methods and the ones that you will find in this book.

SHAKING

This is when you add all the ingredients, with a scoop of ice, to the shaker and then shake vigorously for approximately 5 seconds. The benefit of shaking is that the drink is rapidly mixed, chilled and aerated - after the drink has been shaken, the outside of the shaker will be lightly frosted. Shaking a cocktail also dilutes the drink quite significantly. This dilution is a necessary part of the cocktail-making process and gives shaken recipes the correct balance of taste, strength and temperature.

In addition, shaking can be used to prepare cocktails that include an ingredient, such as egg white, that will not combine effectively with the other ingredients if you use a less vigorous form of mixing.

STIRRING

Once again, you add all the ingredients to a scoop of ice, but this time you combine them in a mixing glass or small jug and then stir the ingredients together using a long-handled bar spoon.

As with shaking, this allows you to blend and chill the ingredients without too much erosion of the ice, so you can control the level of dilution and keep it to a minimum.

This simple but vital technique is essential for drinks that don't need a lot of dilution, such as a classic Dry Martini.

BUILDING

To 'build' a drink, you simply make it in the glass, in the same way that you make a gin and tonic, for example. It is important to follow the instructions for built cocktails to the letter, as the order of ingredients can change from drink to drink and this can affect the finished flavour.

MUDDLING

Muddling is the term used to describe the extraction of the juice or oils from the pulp or skin of a fruit, herb or spice. A muddler is simply a pestle used to crush the ingredient - you can buy a specific cocktail muddler, or just use the end of a wooden spoon.

BLENDING

As the name suggests, this is when the ingredients are combined in a blender! Most blended drinks will have a smooth consistency. The ingredients are usually blended with a scoop of crushed ice and often include items like fresh fruit, which can't be shaken or stirred.

LAYERING

When creating layers in a cocktail you should follow the instructions carefully, putting the heavier spirits or liqueurs into the glass first. If you add them in the wrong order you may find that one layer 'bleeds' into the next, ruining the look of your cocktail. The first, base layer should be poured into the centre of the glass, without getting any down the sides, if possible. To create the second layer, turn a teaspoon upside down, with the tip touching the inside of the glass, then pour the liquid slowly over the back of the spoon (moving it up the glass as the level rises). Repeat with any remaining liquid ingredients, using a clean teaspoon to pour each new layer.

STYLE & FLAIR

Adding ice is incredibly important in the world of cocktail mixing. Get it right and you have the basis of an amazing cocktail, get it wrong and it can make a great drink just average. The ice does two things - during the mixing process it helps to chill and actively mixes the ingredients; once the drink is served it keeps the cocktail cold and prevents too much further dilution. Three types of ice are used in the cocktail recipes here, each with distinctive properties that complement the styles and flavours of the drinks.

CUBED ICE

This is generally used to finish a drink. The more ice you have in your glass, the colder and less diluted your finished cocktail will be. Ice cubes can be made in the freezer in an ice tray - 2-cm/¾-inch cubes are the best size for finishing most drinks. The cubes can be broken down and used to make cracked and crushed ice as necessary.

CRACKED ICE

This is smaller than full ice cubes and is generally used in a shaker to chill the liquid ingredients before you strain them. To make cracked ice from whole cubes, simply wrap the cubes in a clean, dry tea towel and give them a gentle knock with a rolling pin. The ice should be broken into pieces no smaller than half a cube.

CRUSHED ICE

This is perfect for blended drinks as it speeds up the mixing process and freezes the whole concoction very rapidly. Crushed or cracked ice is better for some drinks, as you can pack the glass with the maximum amount of ice (cubes leave greater gaps). To make crushed ice, wrap ice cubes in a clean, dry tea towel and knock a few times with a rolling pin. The cubes should be broken into very small pieces.

Many people consider the decoration to be the thing that defines a cocktail. In some cases, your choice of decoration can reflect the drink itself - think of the Piña Colada with its obligatory pineapple slice. Sometimes the decoration is a vital ingredient but it's usually just added to make the drink look more attractive.

THE FINAL FLOURISH

There are basic guidelines for adding the final
touches to a drink, but ultimately the way in
which you decorate a cocktail will often be
down to your imagination and artistic flair.

One of the simplest rules to follow is to
match the decoration to the main flavours
of the cocktail. Think of your cocktail as a
blank canvas - in this book we recommend some
simple decorations to go with the recipes,
but if you want to have a bit of fun, throw
the rule book in the bin and just have a
go at creating your own.

Remember - enjoy your drinks, don't make
yourself ill and be aware of current government
guidelines on alcohol consumption. Experiment
to your heart's content with this book and get
the maximum pleasure out of your cocktails by
following the recipes, perfecting and using
the tried and tested mixing methods and using
the right glass for whatever cocktail you are
making. Then just decorate and enjoy!

GIN &
VODKA

MARTINI

SERVES 1

INGREDIENTS

4-6 CRACKED ICE CUBES

3 MEASURES GIN

1 TSP DRY VERMOUTH, OR TO TASTE

COCKTAIL OLIVE, TO DECORATE

1. Put the cracked ice cubes into a cocktail shaker.

2. Pour the gin and vermouth over the ice cubes.

3. Shake until well frosted. Strain into a chilled cocktail glass.

4. Decorate with the olive. Serve immediately.

SINGAPORE SLING

SERVES 1

INGREDIENTS

CRACKED ICE CUBES

2 MEASURES GIN

1 MEASURE CHERRY BRANDY

1 MEASURE LEMON JUICE

1 TSP GRENADINE

SODA WATER

LIME PEEL STRIPS AND COCKTAIL CHERRIES, TO DECORATE

1. Put 4-6 cracked ice cubes into a cocktail shaker and pour over the gin.

2. Pour over the cherry brandy, lemon juice and grenadine and shake vigorously until well frosted.

3. Half fill a chilled glass with cracked ice cubes and strain the cocktail over the ice.

4. Top up with soda water and decorate with the lime peel and cherries. Serve immediately.

SERVES 1

TOM COLLINS

1. Put the cracked ice cubes into a cocktail shaker.

2. Pour over the gin, lemon juice and sugar syrup and shake vigorously until well frosted.

3. Strain into a chilled Collins glass.

4. Top up with soda water and decorate with the lemon slices. Serve immediately.

INGREDIENTS

4-6 CRACKED ICE CUBES

3 MEASURES GIN

2 MEASURES LEMON JUICE

½ MEASURE SUGAR SYRUP

SODA WATER

LEMON SLICES,
TO DECORATE

SERVES 1

BELLE COLLINS

1. Muddle the mint sprigs.

2. Place the mint in a chilled tumbler and pour in the gin, lemon juice and sugar syrup.

3. Add the crushed ice cubes to the glass.

4. Top up with sparkling water, stir gently and decorate with more fresh mint. Serve immediately.

INGREDIENTS

2 FRESH MINT SPRIGS, PLUS
EXTRA TO DECORATE

2 MEASURES GIN

1 MEASURE LEMON JUICE

1 TSP SUGAR SYRUP

4-6 CRUSHED ICE CUBES

SPARKLING WATER

GIN RICKEY

SERVES 1

INGREDIENTS

CRACKED ICE

2 MEASURES GIN

1 MEASURE LIME JUICE

SODA WATER

LEMON SLICE, TO DECORATE

1. Fill a chilled highball glass or goblet with cracked ice.

2. Pour over the gin and lime juice.

3. Top up with soda water.

4. Stir gently to mix and decorate with a lemon slice. Serve immediately.

A SLOE KISS

1. Put the cracked ice cubes into a cocktail shaker, pour over the sloe gin, Southern Comfort, vodka and amaretto and shake until well frosted.

2. Strain into a long, chilled glass filled with cracked ice.

3. Splash on the Galliano.

4. Top up with orange juice and decorate with the orange peel. Serve immediately.

SERVES 1

INGREDIENTS

4-6 CRACKED ICE CUBES

½ MEASURE SLOE GIN

½ MEASURE SOUTHERN COMFORT

1 MEASURE VODKA

1 TSP AMARETTO

SPLASH GALLIANO

ORANGE JUICE

ORANGE PEEL TWIST, TO DECORATE

PALM BEACH

1. Shake the gin, rum and pineapple juice vigorously over ice until well frosted.

2. Strain into a chilled glass.

SERVES 1

INGREDIENTS

1 MEASURE GIN

1 MEASURE WHITE RUM

1 MEASURE PINEAPPLE JUICE

CRACKED ICE CUBES

FIREFLY

1. Shake all the liquid ingredients well over ice until frosted.

2. Strain into a chilled cocktail glass and decorate with a twist of orange peel. Serve immediately.

SERVES 1

INGREDIENTS

1 MEASURE GIN

½ MEASURE TEQUILA

½ MEASURE DRY ORANGE CURAÇAO

½ MEASURE LEMON JUICE

DASH EGG WHITE

ICE

ORANGE PEEL, TO DECORATE

INGREDIENTS

1 SUGAR CUBE

1 MEASURE GIN

FRESHLY GRATED NUTMEG

LEMON SLICE, TO SERVE

GIN SLING

1. Place the sugar in an old-fashioned glass and add 125 ml/4 fl oz of hot water. Stir until the sugar is dissolved.

2. Stir in the gin, sprinkle with nutmeg, and serve immediately with a slice of lemon.

SERVES 1

INGREDIENTS

1 MEASURE GIN

1 MEASURE TRIPLE SEC

1 TSP ORANGE JUICE

1 TSP LEMON JUICE

ICE

LEMON PEEL TWIST, TO DECORATE

MAIDEN'S PRAYER

1. Shake the ingredients vigorously over ice until well frosted.

2. Strain into a chilled cocktail glass and decorate with the twist of lemon peel. Serve immediately.

SERVES 1

INGREDIENTS

4 6 CRACKED ICE CUBES

3 MEASURES GIN

1 MEASURE LEMON JUICE

1 TBSP GRENADINE

1 TSP SUGAR SYRUP

SODA WATER

ORANGE WEDGE, TO DECORATE

DAISY

1. Put the cracked ice cubes into a cocktail shaker.

2. Pour over the gin, lemon juice, grenadine and sugar syrup and shake vigorously until well frosted.

3. Strain the cocktail into a chilled highball glass.

4. Top up with soda water, stir gently and decorate with the orange wedge. Serve immediately.

BLOODHOUND

1. Put the gin, sweet vermouth, dry vermouth and strawberries into a blender.

2. Add the cracked ice.

3. Blend until smooth.

4. Pour into a chilled cocktail glass and decorate with the remaining strawberry. Serve immediately.

SERVES 1

INGREDIENTS

2 MEASURES GIN

1 MEASURE SWEET VERMOUTH

1 MEASURE DRY VERMOUTH

3 STRAWBERRIES,
PLUS ONE TO DECORATE

4–6 CRACKED ICE CUBES

SERVES 1

INGREDIENTS

½ MEASURE GIN

½ MEASURE YELLOW
CHARTREUSE

ICE CUBES

ALASKA

1. Shake the gin and Chartreuse over ice until well frosted.

2. Strain into a chilled glass and serve immediately.

SERVES 1

INGREDIENTS

2 MEASURES GIN

1 MEASURE TRIPLE SEC

2 MEASURES ORANGE JUICE

1 MEASURE PINEAPPLE JUICE

ICE

PINEAPPLE SLICES
AND LEAVES, TO DECORATE

HAWAIIAN
ORANGE BLOSSOM

1. Shake the liquid ingredients vigorously over ice until well frosted.

2. Strain into a chilled wine glass and serve immediately decorated with pineapple slices and leaves.

SERVES 1

WEDDING BELLE

1. Shake the liquid ingredients over ice until well frosted.

2. Strain into a chilled glass and serve immediately decorated with a twist of orange peel.

INGREDIENTS

2 MEASURES GIN

2 MEASURES DUBONNET

1 MEASURE CHERRY BRANDY

1 MEASURE ORANGE JUICE

ICE CUBES

ORANGE PEEL, TO DECORATE

SERVES 1

BRIDE'S MOTHER

1. Shake the liquid ingredients vigorously over ice cubes until well frosted.

2. Strain over crushed ice and decorate with grapefruit slices. Serve immediately.

INGREDIENTS

1½ MEASURES SLOE GIN

1 MEASURE GIN

2½ MEASURES GRAPEFRUIT JUICE

½ MEASURE SUGAR SYRUP

ICE CUBES AND CRUSHED ICE

GRAPEFRUIT SLICES, TO DECORATE

SERVES 4

INGREDIENTS

3 MEASURES GRAPEFRUIT JUICE

4 MEASURES GIN

1 MEASURE KIRSCH

4 MEASURES WHITE WINE

½ TSP LEMON ZEST

ICE CUBES

MOONLIGHT

1. Shake all the liquid ingredients vigorously over ice until well frosted. Strain into chilled glasses and serve immediately.

BARTENDER'S TIP

This light cocktail is ideal to make for several people at once.

SERVES 1

INGREDIENTS

2 MEASURES GIN

½ MEASURE MARASCHINO

½ MEASURE GRAPEFRUIT JUICE

ICE CUBES

FRESH MINT SPRIGS, TO DECORATE

SEVENTH HEAVEN

1. Shake all the liquid ingredients vigorously over ice until well frosted.

2. Strain into a chilled cocktail glass. Decorate with fresh mint and serve immediately.

SERVES 1

INGREDIENTS

1 MEASURE GIN

2 MEASURES APRICOT NECTAR OR PEACH NECTAR

1 MEASURE SINGLE CREAM

CRUSHED ICE

½ MEASURE STRAWBERRY SYRUP

FRESH STRAWBERRY AND PEACH SLICES, TO DECORATE

TEARDROP

1. Put the gin, apricot nectar and cream into a blender and blend for 5-10 seconds until thick and frothy.

2. Pour into a long glass filled with crushed ice.

3. Splash the strawberry syrup on the top and decorate with the strawberry and peach slices. Serve immediately.

SERVES 1

INGREDIENTS

1 MEASURE GIN

1 MEASURE PASSION FRUIT NECTAR

4 CUBES MELON OR MANGO

CRACKED ICE

1–2 TSP BLUE CURAÇAO

BLUE BLOODED

1. Put the gin, passion fruit nectar, melon cubes and 4-6 cracked ice cubes into a blender and blend until smooth and frosted.

2. Pour into a tall, chilled glass filled with cracked ice and top with the curaçao. Serve immediately.

SERVES 1

INGREDIENTS

CRACKED ICE

DASH GRENADINE

2 MEASURES GIN

PINEAPPLE JUICE

**PINEAPPLE SLICE,
TO DECORATE**

PUSSYCAT

1. Half fill a chilled tumbler with cracked ice.

2. Dash the grenadine over the ice and add the gin.

3. Top up with pineapple juice and decorate with the pineapple slice. Serve immediately.

SERVES 1

INGREDIENTS

CRUSHED ICE

1 MEASURE GIN

1 MEASURE VODKA

1 MEASURE TEQUILA

**1 MEASURE FRESH LEMON
JUICE**

2 DASHES EGG WHITE

1 MEASURE BLUE CURAÇAO

SODA WATER

LEMON SLICE, TO DECORATE

BLEU BLEU BLEU

1. Put 4-6 crushed ice cubes into a cocktail shaker.

2. Add the gin, vodka, tequila, lemon juice, egg white and curaçao and shake until frosted.

3. Strain the cocktail into a tall glass filled with crushed ice and top up with soda water. Decorate with a lemon slice. Serve immediately.

SERVES 1

INGREDIENTS

2 MEASURES GIN

1 MEASURE LEMON JUICE

1 MEASURE GRENADINE

1 EGG WHITE

ICE

LIME PEEL TWIST,
TO DECORATE

GRAND ROYAL CLOVER CLUB

1. Pour the first four ingredients over ice.

2. Shake vigorously until well frosted and strain into a chilled cocktail glass.

3. Decorate with a twist of lime peel and serve immediately.

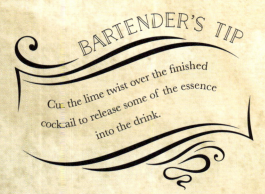

BARTENDER'S TIP

Cut the lime twist over the finished cocktail to release some of the essence into the drink.

THE BLUE TRAIN

1. Pour all of the liquid ingredients into a cocktail shaker filled with ice.

2. Shake vigorously until frosted and strain into a chilled cocktail glass. Serve immediately.

SERVES 1

INGREDIENTS

2 MEASURES GIN

1 MEASURE TRIPLE SEC

1 MEASURE LEMON JUICE

SPLASH BLUE CURAÇAO

CRACKED ICE

SAKETINI

SERVES 1

1. Shake the gin and sake vigorously over ice until well frosted.

2. Strain into a chilled cocktail glass and decorate with a twist of lemon peel. Serve immediately.

INGREDIENTS

3 MEASURES GIN

½ MEASURE SAKE

ICE

LEMON PEEL TWIST, TO DECORATE

GREEN LADY

SERVES 1

1. Shake the liquid ingredients vigorously over ice until well frosted.

2. Strain into a chilled cocktail glass and serve immediately.

INGREDIENTS

2 MEASURES GIN

1 MEASURE GREEN CHARTREUSE

DASH LIME JUICE

ICE

INGREDIENTS

2 MEASURES GIN

1 TSP GRENADINE

1 EGG WHITE

ICE

DASH ORANGE BITTERS

BACHELOR'S BAIT

1. Shake the gin, grenadine and egg white together over ice cubes until well frosted.

2. Add a dash of orange bitters, give the mixture another quick shake and strain into a chilled cocktail glass. Serve immediately.

INGREDIENTS

2 MEASURES GIN

1½ MEASURES MADEIRA

1 TSP GRENADINE

CRACKED ICE

COCKTAIL CHERRIES, TO DECORATE

CREOLE LADY

1. Pour the liquid ingredients over ice in a mixing glass.

2. Stir well to mix, then strain into a chilled glass.

3. Decorate with the cocktail cherries and serve immediately.

SERVES 1

INGREDIENTS

4-6 CRACKED ICE CUBES

2 MEASURES VODKA

1 MEASURE TRIPLE SEC

1 MEASURE LIME JUICE

1 MEASURE CRANBERRY JUICE

ORANGE PEEL STRIP, TO DECORATE

COSMOPOLITAN

1. Put the cracked ice cubes into a cocktail shaker.

2. Pour the liquid ingredients over the ice cubes.

3. Shake vigorously until well frosted.

4. Strain into a chilled cocktail glass and decorate with the orange peel. Serve immediately.

WOO-WOO

1. Half fill a chilled cocktail glass with crushed ice.

2. Pour over the cranberry juice.

3. Add the vodka and peach schnapps.

4. Stir well to mix. Serve immediately.

SERVES 1

INGREDIENTS

CRUSHED ICE

4 MEASURES CRANBERRY JUICE

2 MEASURES VODKA

2 MEASURES PEACH SCHNAPPS

SERVES 1

INGREDIENTS

CRUSHED ICE

1 MEASURE PEACH SCHNAPPS

1 MEASURE VODKA

2 MEASURES FRESH ORANGE JUICE

3 MEASURES CRANBERRY OR PEACH JUICE

DASH LEMON JUICE

ORANGE PEEL TWIST, TO DECORATE

SEX ON THE BEACH

1. Put 4-6 crushed ice cubes into a cocktail shaker and pour over the peach schnapps, vodka, orange juice and cranberry juice.

2. Shake until well frosted and strain into a glass filled with ice.

3. Squeeze over the lemon juice and decorate with the orange peel. Serve immediately.

SERVES 2

INGREDIENTS

4-6 CRACKED ICE CUBES

2 MEASURES VODKA

1 MEASURE PEACH SCHNAPPS

225 ML/8 FL OZ ORANGE JUICE

FUZZY NAVEL

1. Put the cracked ice cubes into a cocktail shaker.

2. Pour the liquid ingredients over the ice cubes and shake vigorously until well frosted.

3. Strain into chilled cocktail glasses. Serve immediately.

SERVES 1

INGREDIENTS

1 TBSP GRANULATED SUGAR

1 TBSP COARSE SALT

1 LIME WEDGE

CRACKED ICE CUBES

2 MEASURES VODKA

GRAPEFRUIT JUICE

SERVES 1

INGREDIENTS

4-6 CRACKED ICE CUBES

1 MEASURE VODKA

1 MEASURE TRIPLE SEC

½ MEASURE FRESH LIME JUICE

**½ MEASURE
FRESH LEMON JUICE**

DRY WHITE WINE, CHILLED

**CUCUMBER AND LIME SLICES,
TO DECORATE**

SALTY DOG

1. Mix the sugar and salt in a saucer. Rub the rim of a chilled cocktail glass with the lime wedge and dip into the sugar and salt mixture to coat.

2. Fill the glass with cracked ice cubes and pour over the vodka.

3. Top up with the grapefruit juice and stir. Serve immediately.

KAMIKAZE

1. Put the cracked ice cubes into a cocktail shaker.

2. Pour over the vodka, triple sec, lime juice and lemon juice and shake until well frosted.

3. Strain into a chilled glass.

4. Top up with wine and decorate with the cucumber and lime slices. Serve immediately.

SERVES 1

INGREDIENTS

CRACKED ICE

3 MEASURES VODKA

8 MEASURES ORANGE JUICE

2 TSP GALLIANO

COCKTAIL CHERRY AND ORANGE SLICE, TO DECORATE

HARVEY WALLBANGER

1. Half fill a tall glass with cracked ice cubes.

2. Pour over the vodka and orange juice.

3. Float the Galliano on top.

4. Decorate with the cherry and the orange slice. Serve immediately.

PEARTINI

SERVES 1

INGREDIENTS

1 TSP CASTER SUGAR

PINCH GROUND CINNAMON

1 LEMON WEDGE

4–6 CRACKED ICE CUBES

1 MEASURE VODKA

1 MEASURE PEAR BRANDY

1. Mix the sugar and cinnamon in a saucer.

2. Rub the rim of a cocktail glass with the lemon wedge.

3. Dip into the sugar and cinnamon mixture, to coat.

4. Put the cracked ice cubes into a cocktail shaker and pour in the vodka and pear brandy. Shake well and strain into the glass. Serve immediately.

SERVES 1

BLACK BEAUTY

1. Stir the vodka and Sambuca with ice in a mixing glass until frosted.

2. Strain into a chilled cocktail glass and decorate with the olive. Serve immediately.

INGREDIENTS

2 MEASURES VODKA

1 MEASURE BLACK SAMBUCA

ICE

BLACK OLIVE, TO DECORATE

SERVES 1

SPOTTED BIKINI

1. Scoop the passion fruit flesh into a jug. Shake the liquid ingredients over ice until well frosted.

2. Strain into a chilled cocktail glass and add the passion fruit at the last minute.

3. Decorate with a slice of lemon peel and serve immediately.

INGREDIENTS

1 RIPE PASSION FRUIT

2 MEASURES VODKA

1 MEASURE WHITE RUM

1 MEASURE COLD MILK

JUICE OF ½ LEMON

ICE

SLICE OF LEMON PEEL, TO DECORATE

SERVES 1

INGREDIENTS

ORANGE WEDGES
CASTER SUGAR
2 MEASURES VODKA, CHILLED

CORDLESS SCREWDRIVER

1. Rub the rim of a chilled shot glass with an orange wedge, then dip into a saucer of sugar to frost.

2. Pour the vodka into the glass.

3. Dip an orange wedge into the sugar.

4. Down the vodka in one go and suck the orange.

SERVES 1

INGREDIENTS

CRACKED ICE
1 MEASURE VODKA
½ MEASURE COINTREAU
1 TBSP BLUE CURAÇAO

BLUE MONDAY

1. Put the cracked ice into a mixing glass or jug and pour in the vodka, Cointreau and curaçao.

2. Stir well, strain into a cocktail glass and serve immediately.

SERVES 1

INGREDIENTS

4-6 CRACKED ICE CUBES

DASH HOT PEPPER SAUCE

DASH WORCESTERSHIRE SAUCE

2 MEASURES VODKA

6 MEASURES TOMATO JUICE

JUICE OF ½ LEMON

PINCH CELERY SALT

PINCH CAYENNE PEPPER

CELERY STICK AND LEMON SLICE, TO DECORATE

BLOODY MARY

1. Put the cracked ice cubes into a cocktail shaker. Dash the hot pepper sauce and Worcestershire sauce over the ice.

2. Add the vodka, tomato juice and lemon juice and shake vigorously until well frosted.

3. Strain into a tall, chilled glass, add the celery salt and cayenne pepper and decorate with the celery stick and lemon slice. Serve immediately.

BARTENDER'S TIP

To make the Canadian favourite Bloody Caesar, simply replace the tomato juice with clamato juice. You can find clamato juice in speciality shops and online.

44

LONG ISLAND ICED TEA

1. Put 4-6 cracked ice cubes into a cocktail shaker. Pour all the liquid ingredients except the cola over the ice, add the sugar and shake vigorously until well frosted.

2. Half fill a tall glass with cracked ice and strain over the cocktail.

3. Top up with cola, decorate with the lime wedge and serve immediately.

SERVES 1

INGREDIENTS

CRACKED ICE

1 MEASURE VODKA

1 MEASURE GIN

1 MEASURE WHITE TEQUILA

1 MEASURE WHITE RUM

½ MEASURE WHITE CRÈME DE MENTHE

2 MEASURES LEMON JUICE

1 TSP CASTER SUGAR

COLA

LIME WEDGE, TO DECORATE

SERVES 1

FLYING GRASSHOPPER

INGREDIENTS

4-6 CRACKED ICE CUBES

1 MEASURE VODKA

1 MEASURE GREEN CRÈME DE MENTHE

1 MEASURE CRÈME DE CACAO

FRESH MINT, TO DECORATE

1. Put the cracked ice cubes into a mixing glass.

2. Pour over the vodka, crème de menthe and crème de cacao and stir well.

3. Strain into a chilled cocktail glass and decorate with a sprig of fresh mint. Serve immediately.

SERVES 1

AURORA BOREALIS

INGREDIENTS

1 MEASURE CHILLED GRAPPA OR VODKA

1 MEASURE CHILLED GREEN CHARTREUSE

½ MEASURE CHILLED ORANGE CURAÇAO

FEW DROPS CHILLED CRÈME DE CASSIS

1. Pour the grappa slowly over the back of a spoon around one side of a well chilled shot glass.

2. Gently pour the Chartreuse around the other side.

3. Pour the curaçao gently into the middle.

4. Add a few drops of crème de cassis. Serve immediately.

SERVES 1

LAST MANGO IN PARIS

INGREDIENTS

2 MEASURES VODKA

1 MEASURE FRAMBOISE

1 MEASURE LIME JUICE

½ MANGO, PEELED, STONED AND CHOPPED

2 HALVED STRAWBERRIES

LIME SLICE, TO DECORATE

1. Mix the ingredients in a blender until slushy.

2. Pour into a chilled glass and decorate with a slice of lime. Serve immediately.

SERVES 1

THUNDERBIRD

1. Pour the vodka into a frosted cocktail glass.

2. Add the other ingredients slowly and stir only once. Serve immediately.

INGREDIENTS

2 MEASURES ICED VODKA

DASH PARFAIT AMOUR

DASH CASSIS

SMALL PIECE OF ORANGE ZEST

1 ROSE OR VIOLET PETAL

SERVES 1

INGREDIENTS

2 MEASURES VODKA

½ MEASURE COCONUT CREAM

2 MEASURES PINEAPPLE JUICE

4–6 CRUSHED ICE CUBES

FRESH PINEAPPLE SLICE, TO DECORATE

MIMI

1. Put the vodka, coconut cream, pineapple juice and crushed ice in a blender.

2. Blend for a few seconds until frothy.

3. Pour into a chilled cocktail glass.

4. Decorate with a slice of pineapple. Serve immediately.

SUNNY BAY

1. Pour the ingredients into a shaker filled with ice.

2. Shake well.

3. Strain into a chilled cocktail glass, and decorate with the cherry on a cocktail stick. Serve immediately.

SERVES 1

INGREDIENTS

1½ MEASURES VODKA

½ MEASURE MELON LIQUEUR

2 MEASURES PINEAPPLE JUICE

CRACKED ICE

COCKTAIL CHERRY,
TO DECORATE

SERVES 1

INGREDIENTS

4–6 CRACKED ICE CUBES

1½ MEASURES VODKA

½ MEASURE CRANBERRY JUICE

PINK GRAPEFRUIT JUICE

SEA BREEZE

1. Put the cracked ice cubes into a cocktail shaker.

2. Pour over the vodka and cranberry juice and shake until frosted.

3. Strain into a chilled tumbler and top up with pink grapefruit juice. Serve immediately.

SERVES 1

INGREDIENTS

CRACKED ICE CUBES

2 MEASURES VODKA

¾ MEASURE ELDERFLOWER CORDIAL

3 MEASURES CRANBERRY JUICE

SODA WATER

LIME SLICE AND LIME PEEL TWIST, TO DECORATE

CRANBERRY COLLINS

1. Put 4-6 cracked ice cubes into a cocktail shaker.

2. Pour over the vodka, elderflower cordial and cranberry juice and shake until well frosted..

3. Strain into a Collins glass filled with cracked ice.

4. Top up with soda water and decorate with the lime slice and peel. Serve immediately.

INGREDIENTS

CRACKED ICE

2 MEASURES VODKA

1 MEASURE LIME JUICE

GINGER BEER

LIME WEDGE, TO DECORATE

MOSCOW MULE

1 Put 4-6 cracked ice cubes into a cocktail shaker.

2 Pour the vodka and lime juice over the ice cubes and shake vigorously until well frosted.

3 Half fill a chilled glass with cracked ice and strain over the cocktail.

4 Top up with ginger beer and decorate with the lime wedge. Serve immediately.

SERVES 1

INGREDIENTS

CRACKED ICE

2 MEASURES VODKA

ORANGE JUICE

ORANGE SLICE, TO DECORATE

SCREWDRIVER

1 Fill a chilled glass with cracked ice. Pour the vodka over the ice.

2 Top up with orange juice and stir well to mix.

3 Decorate with the orange slice. Serve immediately.

METROPOLITAN

1. Rub the rim of a cocktail glass with the lemon wedge.

2. Dip into the sugar, to coat.

3. Put the cracked ice cubes into a cocktail shaker and pour over the liquid ingredients.

4. Cover and shake vigorously until well frosted. Strain into the glass and serve immediately.

SERVES 1

INGREDIENTS

1 LEMON WEDGE

1 TBSP CASTER SUGAR

4-6 CRACKED ICE CUBES

½ MEASURE VODKA

½ MEASURE FRAMBOISE LIQUEUR

½ MEASURE CRANBERRY JUICE

½ MEASURE ORANGE JUICE

VODKA ESPRESSO

1. Put the cracked ice into a cocktail shaker.

2. Pour in the coffee and vodka, add the sugar and shake vigorously until well frosted.

3. Strain into a chilled cocktail glass.

4. Float the Amarula on top. Serve immediately.

SERVES 1

INGREDIENTS

4-6 CRACKED ICE CUBES

2 MEASURES ESPRESSO OR OTHER STRONG BLACK COFFEE, COOLED

1 MEASURE VODKA

2 TSP CASTER SUGAR

1 MEASURE AMARULA

RUM, WHISKIES & BRANDY

SERVES 1

DAIQUIRI

1. Put the cracked ice cubes into a cocktail shaker.

2. Pour the rum, sugar water and lime juice over the ice cubes. Shake vigorously until well frosted.

3. Strain into a chilled cocktail glass and decorate with a wedge of lime. Serve immediately.

INGREDIENTS

4-6 CRACKED ICE CUBES

2 MEASURES WHITE RUM

½ TSP CASTER SUGAR, DISSOLVED IN

1 TBSP BOILING WATER

¼ MEASURE LIME JUICE

LIME WEDGE, TO DECORATE

SERVES 1

BANANA COLADA

1. Whizz the crushed ice in a blender with the white rum, pineapple juice, Malibu and sliced banana.

2. Blend until smooth, then pour, without straining, into a chilled highball glass and serve immediately with pineapple wedges and a straw.

INGREDIENTS

4-6 ICE CUBES, CRUSHED

2 MEASURES WHITE RUM

4 MEASURES PINEAPPLE JUICE

1 MEASURE MALIBU

1 BANANA, PEELED AND SLICED

PINEAPPLE WEDGES

SERVES 1

HURRICANE

1. Put the cracked ice cubes into a cocktail shaker.

2. Add the rum, lemon juice and orange and passion fruit juice, and shake until well combined.

3. Pour the cocktail into a tall, chilled glass and top up with soda water.

4. Decorate with the orange slices and cherries and serve immediately.

INGREDIENTS

4-6 CRACKED ICE CUBES

4 MEASURES DARK RUM

1 MEASURE LEMON JUICE

2 MEASURES ORANGE AND PASSION FRUIT JUICE

SODA WATER

ORANGE SLICES AND COCKTAIL CHERRIES, TO DECORATE

SERVES 1

STRAWBERRY COLADA

1. Put the crushed ice in a blender. Add the rum, pineapple juice and coconut cream.

2. Hull the strawberries and add to the blender. Blend until smooth and pour, without straining, into a tall, chilled tumbler.

3. Decorate with the pineapple wedge and strawberry and serve immediately.

INGREDIENTS

4-6 CRUSHED ICE CUBES

3 MEASURES GOLDEN RUM

4 MEASURES PINEAPPLE JUICE

1 MEASURE COCONUT CREAM

6 STRAWBERRIES

PINEAPPLE WEDGE AND HALVED STRAWBERRY, TO DECORATE

SERVES 1

INGREDIENTS

4-6 CRUSHED ICE CUBES

2 MEASURES WHITE RUM

1 MEASURE DARK RUM

3 MEASURES PINEAPPLE JUICE

2 MEASURES COCONUT CREAM

COCKTAIL CHERRY AND PINEAPPLE WEDGE, TO DECORATE

PIÑA COLADA

1. Put the crushed ice cubes in a blender. Pour over the white rum, dark rum and pineapple juice.

2. Add the coconut cream to the blender and blend until smooth.

3. Pour, without straining, into a chilled glass.

4. Decorate with the cocktail cherry and the pineapple wedge.

5. Serve immediately.

CLUB MOJITO

1. Put the sugar syrup, mint leaves and lime juice into a lowball glass.

2. Muddle the mint leaves, then add the cracked ice cubes and the rum.

3. Top up with soda water.

4. Finish with the Angostura bitters and decorate with the remaining mint leaves.

5. Serve immediately.

SERVES 1

INGREDIENTS

1 TSP SUGAR SYRUP

6 FRESH MINT LEAVES, PLUS EXTRA TO DECORATE

JUICE OF ½ LIME

4–6 CRACKED ICE CUBES

2 MEASURES JAMAICAN RUM

SODA WATER

DASH ANGOSTURA BITTERS

SERVES 1

INGREDIENTS

4-6 CRUSHED ICE CUBES

1 MEASURE WHITE RUM

1 MEASURE MANDARIN BRANDY

1 MEASURE FRESH ORANGE JUICE

1 MEASURE PINEAPPLE JUICE

SPLASH GRENADINE

FRESH PINEAPPLE SLICE AND COCKTAIL CHERRY, TO DECORATE

BAJAN SUN

1. Put the crushed ice into a cocktail shaker.

2. Pour over the rum, brandy, orange juice and pineapple juice.

3. Add the grenadine and shake vigorously.

4. Strain into a tall, chilled glass and decorate with the pineapple slice and cocktail cherry. Serve immediately.

SERVES 1

INGREDIENTS

4-5 CRACKED ICE CUBES

2 MEASURES DARK RUM

1 MEASURE SOUTHERN COMFORT

1 MEASURE LEMON JUICE

1 TSP BROWN SUGAR

SPARKLING WATER

1 TSP RUBY PORT

PLANTATION PUNCH

1. Put the cracked ice cubes into a cocktail shaker. Add the rum, Southern Comfort, lemon juice and brown sugar.

2. Shake vigorously until well frosted. Strain into a tall, chilled glass. Top up with sparkling water.

3. Float the port on top by pouring it gently over the back of a teaspoon. Serve immediately.

SERVES 1

OCEAN BREEZE

1. Put the crushed ice into a cocktail shaker.

2. Pour over the white rum, amaretto, blue curaçao and pineapple juice and shake well.

3. Strain into a tall, chilled glass and top up with soda water. Serve immediately.

INGREDIENTS

4-6 CRUSHED ICE CUBES

1 MEASURE WHITE RUM

1 MEASURE AMARETTO

½ MEASURE BLUE CURAÇAO

½ MEASURE PINEAPPLE JUICE

SODA WATER

SERVES 1

BLUE HAWAIIAN

1. Put the crushed ice in a cocktail shaker.

2. Pour over the liquid ingredients. Shake vigorously until well frosted and strain into a chilled wine glass.

3. Decorate with the pineapple wedge. Serve immediately.

INGREDIENTS

4-6 CRUSHED ICE CUBES

2 MEASURES BACARDI RUM

½ MEASURE BLUE CURAÇAO

1 MEASURE PINEAPPLE JUICE

½ MEASURE COCONUT CREAM

PINEAPPLE WEDGE, TO DECORATE

MAI TAI

SERVES 1

INGREDIENTS

4-6 CRACKED ICE CUBES

1 MEASURE WHITE RUM

1 MEASURE DARK RUM

1 MEASURE ORANGE CURAÇAO

1 MEASURE LIME JUICE

1 TBSP ORGEAT SYRUP

1 TBSP GRENADINE

TO DECORATE

PINEAPPLE WEDGE

PINEAPPLE LEAVES

COCKTAIL CHERRY

ORANGE PEEL TWIST

1. Put the cracked ice cubes into a cocktail shaker. Pour over the white rum, dark rum, curaçao, lime juice, orgeat syrup and grenadine.

2. Shake vigorously until well frosted and strain into a chilled glass.

3. Decorate with the pineapple wedge, leaves, cocktail cherry and orange peel. Serve immediately.

SERVES 3

INGREDIENTS

4-6 CRUSHED ICE CUBES

2 MEASURES DARK RUM

2 MEASURES WHITE RUM

1 MEASURE GOLDEN RUM

1 MEASURE TRIPLE SEC

1 MEASURE LIME JUICE

1 MEASURE ORANGE JUICE

1 MEASURE PINEAPPLE JUICE

1 MEASURE GUAVA JUICE

1 TBSP GRENADINE

1 TBSP ORGEAT SYRUP

1 TSP PERNOD

FRESH MINT SPRIGS AND PINEAPPLE WEDGES, TO DECORATE

ZOMBIE

1. Put the crushed ice cubes into a cocktail shaker.

2. Pour over the liquid ingredients and shake vigorously until well frosted.

3. Pour the cocktail into chilled glasses and decorate with the fresh mint and the pineapple wedges. Serve immediately.

SERVES 1

INGREDIENTS

CRACKED ICE

2 MEASURES WHITE RUM

COLA

LIME WEDGE, TO DECORATE

CUBA LIBRE

1. Half fill a highball glass with cracked ice.

2. Pour over the rum and top up with cola.

3. Stir gently to mix and decorate with the lime wedge. Serve immediately.

SERVES 1

INGREDIENTS

4-6 CRACKED ICE CUBES

2 MEASURES WHITE RUM

1 MEASURE LIME JUICE

1 TBSP PINEAPPLE JUICE

1 TSP TRIPLE SEC

PINEAPPLE WEDGES, TO DECORATE

CUBAN SPECIAL

1. Put the cracked ice cubes into a cocktail shaker.

2. Pour over the rum, lime juice, pineapple juice and triple sec. Shake vigorously until well frosted. Strain into a chilled cocktail glass.

3. Decorate with the pineapple wedges and serve immediately.

SERVES 8

RUM NOGGIN

1. Whisk the eggs in a punch bowl with the sugar and a little nutmeg.

2. Whisk in the rum and gradually stir in the milk.

3. Warm through gently, if you wish, and serve immediately in small heatproof glasses or mugs, sprinkled with nutmeg.

INGREDIENTS

6 EGGS

4–5 TSP ICING SUGAR

FRESHLY GRATED NUTMEG, PLUS EXTRA FOR SPRINKLING

475 ML/16 FL OZ DARK RUM

1.2 LITRES/2 PINTS MILK, WARMED

SERVES 1

RUM COBBLER

1. Put the sugar into a chilled goblet. Add the sparkling water and stir until the sugar has dissolved.

2. Fill the glass with ice and pour in the rum. Stir well and decorate with a lime slice and an orange slice.
Serve immediately.

INGREDIENTS

1 TSP ICING SUGAR

2 MEASURES SPARKLING WATER

CRACKED ICE

2 MEASURES WHITE RUM

LIME SLICE AND ORANGE SLICE, TO DECORATE

FROZEN PEACH DAIQUIRI

1. Put the crushed ice and the peach into a blender.

2. Add the rum, lime juice and sugar syrup and blend until slushy.

3. Pour into a chilled cocktail glass.

4. Decorate with the peach slice.

5. Serve immediately.

SERVES 1

INGREDIENTS

4-6 CRUSHED ICE CUBES

½ PEACH, STONED AND CHOPPED

2 MEASURES WHITE RUM

1 MEASURE LIME JUICE

1 TSP SUGAR SYRUP

PEACH SLICE, TO DECORATE

RUM COOLER

1. Put 2-4 cracked ice cubes, the rum, pineapple juice and banana into a blender.

2. Add the lime juice and blend for about 1 minute or until smooth.

3. Fill a chilled glass with cracked ice and pour over the cocktail.

4. Decorate with the lime peel.

5. Serve immediately.

SERVES 1

INGREDIENTS

CRACKED ICE

1½ MEASURES WHITE RUM

1½ MEASURES PINEAPPLE JUICE

1 BANANA, PEELED AND SLICED

JUICE OF 1 LIME

LIME PEEL TWIST, TO DECORATE

SERVES 1

WHISKEY SOUR

1. Put the cracked ice cubes into a cocktail shaker and pour over the whiskey.

2. Add the lime juice and sugar and shake well.

3. Strain into a cocktail glass and decorate with the slice of lime and a cherry. Serve immediately.

INGREDIENTS

4-6 CRACKED ICE CUBES

2 MEASURES BLENDED WHISKEY

1 MEASURE LIME JUICE

1 TSP ICING SUGAR OR
SUGAR SYRUP

**LIME SLICE AND COCKTAIL
CHERRY, TO DECORATE**

SERVES 1

WHISKEY RICKEY

1. Put the crushed ice into a chilled highball glass.

2. Pour over the whiskey and lime juice and top up with soda water.

3. Stir gently to mix, decorate with the lime slice and serve immediately.

INGREDIENTS

4-6 CRUSHED ICE CUBES

2 MEASURES BLENDED WHISKEY

1 MEASURE LIME JUICE

SODA WATER

LIME SLICE, TO DECORATE

SERVES 1

HIGHLAND FLING

1. Put the cracked ice into a mixing glass.

2. Pour over the Angostura bitters. Pour in the whisky and vermouth and stir well to mix.

3. Strain into a chilled glass and decorate with the olive. Serve immediately.

INGREDIENTS

4-6 CRACKED ICE CUBES

DASH ANGOSTURA BITTERS

2 MEASURES SCOTCH WHISKY

1 MEASURE SWEET VERMOUTH

COCKTAIL OLIVE, TO DECORATE

SERVES 1

WHISKEY SLING

1. Put the sugar into a mixing glass.

2. Add the lemon juice and water and stir until the sugar has dissolved.

3. Pour in the whiskey and stir to mix.

4. Half fill a small chilled tumbler with cracked ice and strain the cocktail over it.

5. Decorate with the orange wedge and serve immediately.

INGREDIENTS

1 TSP ICING SUGAR

1 MEASURE LEMON JUICE

1 TSP WATER

2 MEASURES BLENDED WHISKEY

CRACKED ICE

ORANGE WEDGE, TO DECORATE

SERVES 1

INGREDIENTS

4-6 CRACKED ICE CUBES

2 MEASURES SCOTCH WHISKY

1½ MEASURES DRY VERMOUTH

2 MEASURES PINK GRAPEFRUIT
JUICE

**ORANGE PEEL STRIP, TO
DECORATE**

MIAMI BEACH

1. Put the cracked ice cubes into a
cocktail shaker.

2. Pour over the whisky, vermouth
and grapefruit juice.

3. Shake vigorously until well
frosted. Strain into a chilled
cocktail glass.

4. Decorate with the orange peel
strip and serve immediately.

BOSTON SOUR

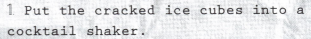

1. Put the cracked ice cubes into a cocktail shaker.

2. Pour over the lemon juice, whiskey and sugar syrup.

3. Add the egg white.

4. Shake until chilled. Strain into a cocktail glass and decorate with the lemon slice and a cocktail cherry. Serve immediately.

SERVES 1

INGREDIENTS

4-6 CRACKED ICE CUBES

1 MEASURE LEMON JUICE OR LIME JUICE

2 MEASURES BLENDED WHISKEY

1 TSP SUGAR SYRUP

1 EGG WHITE

LEMON SLICE AND COCKTAIL CHERRY, TO DECORATE

INGREDIENTS

½ TSP ICING SUGAR

1 MEASURE GINGER ALE

CRACKED ICE

2 MEASURES BLENDED WHISKEY

SPARKLING WATER

LEMON PEEL TWIST, TO DECORATE

KLONDIKE COOLER

1. Put the sugar into a chilled tumbler and add the ginger ale. Stir until the sugar has dissolved.

2. Fill the glass with cracked ice. Pour over the whiskey.

3. Top up with sparkling water. Stir gently and decorate with the lemon peel. Serve immediately.

INGREDIENTS

4–6 CRACKED ICE CUBES

1 MEASURE IRISH WHISKEY

1 MEASURE DRY VERMOUTH

3 DASHES GREEN CHARTREUSE

3 DASHES CRÈME DE MENTHE

SHAMROCK

1. Put the cracked ice into a mixing glass.

2. Pour over the whiskey, vermouth and Chartreuse. Stir until well frosted.

3. Strain into a chilled cocktail glass, pour over the crème de menthe and stir. Serve immediately.

MANHATTAN

SERVES 1

INGREDIENTS

4-6 CRACKED ICE CUBES

DASH ANGOSTURA BITTERS

3 MEASURES RYE WHISKEY

1 MEASURE SWEET VERMOUTH

COCKTAIL CHERRY, TO DECORATE

1. Put the cracked ice cubes into a cocktail shaker.

2. Pour the liquid ingredients over the ice cubes and shake vigorously until well frosted.

3. Strain into a chilled cocktail glass and decorate with the cherry. Serve immediately.

OLD-FASHIONED

SERVES 1

INGREDIENTS

1 SUGAR CUBE

DASH ANGOSTURA BITTERS

1 TSP WATER

2 MEASURES BOURBON OR RYE WHISKEY

4-6 CRACKED ICE CUBES

LEMON PEEL TWIST, TO DECORATE

1. Place the sugar cube in a small, chilled lowball glass.

2. Add the Angostura bitters and water. Stir until the sugar has dissolved.

3. Pour in the bourbon and stir.

4. Add the cracked ice cubes and decorate with the lemon peel. Serve immediately.

SERVES 1

INGREDIENTS

4-6 ICE CUBES

2 MEASURES BOURBON

1 TSP SUGAR SYRUP

SODA WATER

1 TBSP RUBY PORT

FRESHLY GRATED NUTMEG,
TO DECORATE

WHISKEY SANGAREE

1. Put the ice in a chilled tumbler.

2. Pour over the bourbon and sugar syrup. Top up with soda water.

3. Stir gently to mix, then float the port on top. Sprinkle over some of the grated nutmeg. Serve immediately.

BARTENDER'S TIP

Instead of bourbon whiskey, try a blended whiskey, or indeed any whiskey of your choice in this cocktail classic.

PINK HEATHER

SERVES 1

INGREDIENTS

1 MEASURE SCOTCH WHISKY

1 MEASURE STRAWBERRY LIQUEUR

CHILLED SPARKLING WINE

FRESH STRAWBERRY, TO DECORATE

1. Pour the whisky and the strawberry liqueur into a chilled champagne flute.

2. Top up with chilled sparkling wine and decorate with a strawberry. Serve immediately.

FLYING SCOTSMAN

1. Put some crushed ice into a blender.

2. Dash Angostura bitters over the ice, and add the whisky, vermouth and sugar syrup.

3. Blend until slushy and pour into a small chilled tumbler. Serve immediately.

INGREDIENTS

CRUSHED ICE
DASH ANGOSTURA BITTERS
2 MEASURES SCOTCH WHISKY
1 MEASURE SWEET VERMOUTH
¼ TSP SUGAR SYRUP

BEADLESTONE

1. Put some cracked ice into a mixing glass and pour the whisky and vermouth over the ice.

2. Stir well to mix and strain into a chilled cocktail glass. Serve immediately.

INGREDIENTS

CRACKED ICE
2 MEASURES SCOTCH WHISKY
1½ MEASURES DRY VERMOUTH

THISTLE

1. Put some cracked ice into a mixing glass.

2. Dash Angostura bitters over the ice and pour in the whisky and vermouth.

3. Stir well to mix and strain into a chilled cocktail glass. Serve immediately.

INGREDIENTS

CRACKED ICE

DASH ANGOSTURA BITTERS

2 MEASURES SCOTCH WHISKY

1½ MEASURES SWEET VERMOUTH

COLLEEN

1. Shake the liquid ingredients vigorously over ice until well frosted.

2. Strain into a chilled cocktail glass. Serve immediately.

INGREDIENTS

2 MEASURES IRISH WHISKEY

1 MEASURE IRISH MIST

1 MEASURE TRIPLE SEC

1 TSP LEMON JUICE

ICE

SERVES 1

INGREDIENTS

¹/₃ MEASURE BRANDY
¹/₃ MEASURE FERNET BRANCA
¹/₃ MEASURE CRÈME DE MENTHE
ICE

THE REVIVER

1. Shake the liquids well over ice until frosted.

2. Strain into a wine glass and drink as quickly as possible.

BARTENDER'S TIP

This cocktail, as its name suggests, is supposed to revive after a night of heavy drinking!

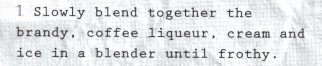

MIDNIGHT COWBOY

1. Slowly blend together the brandy, coffee liqueur, cream and ice in a blender until frothy.

2. Pour into a chilled cocktail glass. Top up with cola and serve immediately.

SERVES 1

INGREDIENTS

1 MEASURE BRANDY

½ MEASURE COFFEE LIQUEUR

½ MEASURE CREAM, CHILLED

CRUSHED ICE

COLA

INGREDIENTS

2 MEASURES BRANDY

1 MEASURE APRICOT BRANDY

1 MEASURE LIME JUICE

1 TSP WHITE RUM

ICE

CUBAN

1. Pour the liquid ingredients over ice and shake vigorously until well frosted.

2. Strain into a chilled cocktail glass and serve immediately.

INGREDIENTS

1 MEASURE LEMON OR LIME JUICE

2½ MEASURES BRANDY

1 TSP ICING SUGAR OR SUGAR SYRUP

ICE

LIME SLICE AND COCKTAIL CHERRY, TO DECORATE

BRANDY SOUR

1. Shake the lemon juice, brandy and sugar well over ice and strain into a cocktail glass.

2. Decorate with a lime slice and a cherry and serve immediately.

SERVES 1

SIDECAR

1. Put the cracked ice cubes into a cocktail shaker. Pour the liquid ingredients over the ice cubes.

2. Shake vigorously until well frosted.

3. Strain into a chilled cocktail glass and decorate with the orange peel. Serve immediately.

INGREDIENTS

4-6 CRACKED ICE CUBES

2 MEASURES BRANDY

1 MEASURE TRIPLE SEC

1 MEASURE LEMON JUICE

ORANGE PEEL TWIST, TO DECORATE

SERVES 1

BRANDY JULEP

1. Fill a chilled lowball glass with cracked ice.

2. Add the brandy, sugar syrup and mint leaves, and stir well to mix.

3. Decorate the cocktail with a sprig of fresh mint and a slice of lemon. Serve immediately.

INGREDIENTS

CRACKED ICE

2 MEASURES BRANDY

1 TSP SUGAR SYRUP

4 FRESH MINT LEAVES

FRESH MINT SPRIG AND LEMON SLICE, TO DECORATE

SERVES 1

INGREDIENTS

2 MEASURES APRICOT BRANDY

1 MEASURE DRY VERMOUTH

2 MEASURES ORANGE JUICE

DASH GRENADINE

ICE

PINK WHISKERS

1. Shake the liquid ingredients vigorously over ice until well frosted.

2. Strain the mixture into a chilled cocktail glass and serve immediately.

BARTENDER'S TIP

Float 2 tablespoons of port on top for an extra depth and flavour.

SERVES 1

INGREDIENTS

2 MEASURES BRANDY

1 MEASURE VAN DER HUM

1 MEASURE TIA MARIA

1 TSP CREAM

ICE

GRATED CHOCOLATE, TO DECORATE

FIRST NIGHT

1. Shake the liquid ingredients together over ice.

2. Strain into a chilled cocktail glass and decorate with a little grated chocolate. Serve immediately.

SERVES 1

INGREDIENTS

CRACKED ICE

1½ MEASURES BRANDY

½ MEASURE CHERRY BRANDY

½ MEASURE PLUM BRANDY

**COCKTAIL CHERRIES,
TO DECORATE**

HEAVENLY

1. Put the ice in a mixing glass.

2. Pour the liquid ingredients over the ice and stir well to mix.

3. Strain into a chilled glass and decorate with cocktail cherries. Serve immediately.

CHERRY KITSCH

1. Shake the cherry brandy, pineapple juice, kirsch and egg white well over ice until frosted.

2. Pour into a chilled tall thin glass and top with a frozen cocktail cherry. Serve immediately.

SERVES 1

INGREDIENTS

1 MEASURE CHERRY BRANDY

2 MEASURES PINEAPPLE JUICE

½ MEASURE KIRSCH

1 EGG WHITE

CRUSHED ICE

FROZEN COCKTAIL CHERRY,
TO DECORATE

GODDAUGHTER

1. Put some crushed ice into a blender and add the apple brandy, amaretto and apple sauce.

2. Blend until smooth, then pour the mixture, without straining, into a chilled glass.

3. Sprinkle with ground cinnamon and serve immediately.

SERVES 1

INGREDIENTS

CRUSHED ICE

2 MEASURES APPLE BRANDY

1 MEASURE AMARETTO

1 TSP APPLE SAUCE

GROUND CINNAMON, TO DECORATE

BEAGLE

1. Put cracked ice into a mixing glass.

2. Dash kümmel and lemon juice over the ice and pour in the brandy and cranberry juice.

3. Stir well to mix, strain into a chilled cocktail glass and serve immediately.

SERVES 1

INGREDIENTS

CRACKED ICE

DASH KÜMMEL

DASH LEMON JUICE

2 MEASURES BRANDY

1 MEASURE CRANBERRY JUICE

SERVES 1

INGREDIENTS

4-6 CRACKED ICE CUBES

1 MEASURE BRANDY

1 MEASURE DARK CRÈME
DE CACAO

1 MEASURE DOUBLE CREAM

**FRESHLY GRATED NUTMEG,
TO DECORATE**

BRANDY ALEXANDER

1. Put the cracked ice cubes into a cocktail shaker.

2. Pour over the brandy, crème de cacao and cream and shake vigorously until well frosted.

3. Strain into a chilled cocktail glass. Sprinkle over the grated nutmeg and serve immediately.

BARTENDER'S TIP

This is the perfect after dinner cocktail to serve with a creamy, chocolate dessert.

HOT BRANDY CHOCOLATE

1. Heat the milk in a small pan to just below boiling point.

2. Add the chocolate and sugar and stir over a low heat until the chocolate has melted.

3. Pour into four warmed heatproof glasses, then pour 1 measure of the brandy over the back of a spoon on top of each.

4. Add the whipped cream and sprinkle over the grated nutmeg. Serve immediately.

SERVES 4

INGREDIENTS

1 LITRE/1¾ PINTS MILK

115 G/4 OZ PLAIN CHOCOLATE, BROKEN INTO PIECES

2 TBSP SUGAR

4 MEASURES BRANDY

6 TBSP WHIPPED CREAM

FRESHLY GRATED NUTMEG OR COCOA POWDER, FOR SPRINKLING

BUBBLES
(BOTH NAUGHTY & NICE)

SERVES 1

KIR ROYALE

1. Put the cassis into the bottom of a champagne flute.

2. Add the brandy. Top up with champagne.

3. Decorate with the mint sprig and serve immediately.

INGREDIENTS

FEW DROPS CRÈME DE CASSIS, OR TO TASTE

½ MEASURE BRANDY

CHILLED CHAMPAGNE

FRESH MINT SPRING, TO DECORATE

SERVES 1

DISCO DANCER

1. Shake the first three ingredients well over ice.

2. Pour into a chilled glass and top up with sparkling wine to taste. Serve immediately.

INGREDIENTS

1 MEASURE CRÈME DE BANANE

1 MEASURE RUM

FEW DROPS ANGOSTURA BITTERS

ICE

SPARKLING WHITE WINE

SERVES 1

DIAMOND FIZZ

1. Shake the gin, lemon juice and sugar syrup over ice until well frosted.

2. Strain into a chilled flute. Top up with chilled champagne and serve immediately.

INGREDIENTS

2 MEASURES GIN

½ MEASURE LEMON JUICE

1 TSP SUGAR SYRUP

ICE

CHILLED CHAMPAGNE

SERVES 1

CHAMPAGNE SIDECAR

1. Shake the bourbon, Cointreau and lemon juice over ice and strain into a chilled flute.

2. Top up with chilled champagne and serve immediately.

INGREDIENTS

1½ MEASURES BOURBON

1 MEASURE COINTREAU

¼ MEASURE LEMON JUICE

ICE

CHILLED CHAMPAGNE

CHAMPAGNE COCKTAIL

SERVES 1

INGREDIENTS

1 SUGAR CUBE
2 DASHES ANGOSTURA BITTERS
1 MEASURE BRANDY
CHILLED CHAMPAGNE

1. Place the sugar cube in the bottom of a chilled champagne flute.

2. Add the Angostura bitters and the brandy.

3. Top up with champagne and serve immediately.

CHAMPAGNE PICK-ME-UP

1. Put the cracked ice cubes into a cocktail shaker.

2. Pour over the brandy, orange juice, lemon juice and grenadine and shake vigorously until well frosted.

3. Strain into a chilled wine glass, top up with champagne and serve immediately.

SERVES 1

INGREDIENTS

4-6 CRACKED ICE CUBES

2 MEASURES BRANDY

1 MEASURE ORANGE JUICE

1 MEASURE LEMON JUICE

DASH GRENADINE

CHILLED CHAMPAGNE

SERVES 1

BUCK'S FIZZ

1. Half fill a chilled flute with orange juice, then gently pour in the chilled champagne. Serve immediately.

INGREDIENTS

2 MEASURES CHILLED FRESH ORANGE JUICE

2 MEASURES CHILLED CHAMPAGNE

SERVES 1

DUKE

1. Shake the triple sec, lemon juice, orange juice, egg white and maraschino liqueur vigorously over cracked ice until well frosted.

2. Strain into a chilled wine glass and top up with chilled champagne. Serve immediately.

INGREDIENTS

1 MEASURE TRIPLE SEC

½ MEASURE LEMON JUICE

½ MEASURE ORANGE JUICE

1 EGG WHITE

DASH MARASCHINO LIQUEUR

CRACKED ICE CUBES

CHILLED CHAMPAGNE OR SPARKLING WINE

KISMET

1. Pour the gin and brandy into a chilled flute.

2. Trickle the ginger syrup slowly down the glass and then top up with champagne. Decorate with a slice of mango and serve immediately.

INGREDIENTS

1 MEASURE GIN

1 MEASURE APRICOT BRANDY

½ TSP STEM GINGER SYRUP

CHILLED CHAMPAGNE

FRESH MANGO SLICES, TO DECORATE

LONDON FRENCH 75

1. Shake the gin and lemon juice vigorously over cracked ice until well frosted.

2. Strain into a chilled glass and top up with champagne. Serve immediately.

INGREDIENTS

2 MEASURES LONDON GIN

1 MEASURE LEMON JUICE

CRACKED ICE CUBES

CHILLED CHAMPAGNE

SERVES 1

INGREDIENTS

1 LEMON WEDGE

CASTER SUGAR

1 MEASURE PEACH JUICE

3 MEASURES CHILLED CHAMPAGNE

BELLINI

1. Rub the rim of a chilled champagne flute with the lemon wedge.

2. Put the sugar in a saucer, then dip the rim of the flute in it.

3. Pour the peach juice into the flute.

4. Top up with the champagne.

5. Serve immediately.

MIMOSA

1 Put the cracked ice cubes into a cocktail shaker.

2 Scoop out the passion-fruit flesh into the shaker.

3 Add the curaçao and shake until frosted.

4 Strain into a chilled champagne flute, top up with champagne and decorate with the star fruit slice.

5 Serve immediately.

SERVES 1

INGREDIENTS

CRACKED ICE

1 PASSION FRUIT

½ MEASURE ORANGE CURAÇAO

CHILLED CHAMPAGNE

STAR FRUIT SLICE, TO DECORATE

SERVES 1

INGREDIENTS

½ MEASURE GRAPEFRUIT JUICE

¼ MEASURE TRIPLE SEC

¼ MEASURE MANDARIN LIQUEUR

ICE

CHILLED CHAMPAGNE

FROZEN CITRUS FRUIT SLICES,
TO DECORATE

SAN REMO

1. Mix the first three ingredients with ice in a tall glass.

2. Top up with champagne and decorate with slices of frozen fruit. Serve immediately.

SERVES 1

INGREDIENTS

1 MEASURE GOLDEN RUM

½ MEASURE COINTREAU

CHILLED CHAMPAGNE

SPARKLING GOLD

1. Pour the rum and liqueur into a chilled champagne flute.

2. Top up with champagne. Serve immediately.

SERVES 1

INGREDIENTS

½ MEASURE COGNAC OR BRANDY

½ MEASURE PEACH LIQUEUR, PEACH BRANDY OR SCHNAPPS

JUICE OF 1 PASSION FRUIT, SIEVED

1 ICE CUBE

CHILLED CHAMPAGNE

THE BENTLEY

1. Mix the first three ingredients gently together in a chilled glass.

2. Add one ice cube and slowly pour in champagne to taste. Serve immediately.

SERVES 24

INGREDIENTS

6 MEASURES IRISH MIST

450 G/1 LB RASPBERRIES

55 G/2 OZ CRUSHED ICE

4 BOTTLES SPARKLING DRY WHITE WINE, WELL CHILLED

24 RASPBERRIES, TO DECORATE

RASPBERRY MIST

1. Blend the Irish Mist and raspberries in a blender with the crushed ice.

2. When lightly frozen, strain between chilled champagne glasses and top up with wine.

3. Top each glass with a raspberry and serve immediately.

WILD SILK

1. Set aside 2 unbruised raspberries. Blend the remainder with the cream, framboise and a little ice in a blender until frosted and slushy.

2. Pour into chilled glasses and top up with champagne.

3. Float a raspberry on top and serve immediately.

SERVES 2

INGREDIENTS

A FEW RASPBERRIES

½ MEASURE CREAM

1 MEASURE FRAMBOISE OR RASPBERRY SYRUP

CRUSHED ICE

CHILLED CHAMPAGNE

BLACK VELVET

1. Half fill a tumbler with stout, then very slowly pour in an equal quantity of wine over the back of a spoon that is just touching the top of the stout and the edge of the glass. Serve immediately.

SERVES 1

INGREDIENTS

CHILLED STOUT

CHILLED SPARKLING WHITE WINE

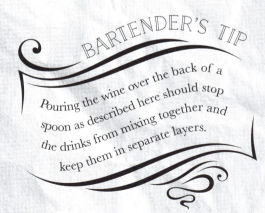

BARTENDER'S TIP

Pouring the wine over the back of a spoon as described here should stop the drinks from mixing together and keep them in separate layers.

SERVES 1

ROYAL JULEP

1. In a small glass, crush the sugar and mint together with a little of the whiskey.

2. When the sugar has dissolved, strain it into a chilled glass with the rest of the whiskey, and top up with champagne.

3. Decorate with a mint sprig and serve immediately.

INGRED ENTS

1 SUGAR LUMP

3 SPRIGS FRESH MINT, PLUS EXTRA TO DECORATE

1 MEASURE JACK DANIELS WHISKEY

CHILLED CHAMPAGNE

SERVES 1

CARIBBEAN CHAMPAGNE

1. Pour the rum and crème de banane into a chilled flute and top up with champagne.

2. Stir gently to mix and decorate with slices of banana. Serve immediately.

INGREDIENTS

½ MEASURE WHITE RUM

½ MEASURE CRÈME DE BANANE

CHILLED CHAMPAGNE

BANANA SLICES, TO DECORATE

SERVES 1

JADE

1. Shake the Midori, curaçao, lime juice and Angostura bitters vigorously over ice until well frosted.

2. Strain into a chilled flute. Top up with chilled champagne and decorate with a slice of lime. Serve immediately.

INGREDIENTS

¼ MEASURE MIDORI

¼ MEASURE BLUE CURAÇAO

¼ MEASURE LIME JUICE

DASH ANGOSTURA BITTERS

CRACKED ICE

CHILLED CHAMPAGNE

LIME SLICE, TO DECORATE

SERVES 1

UNDER THE BOARDWALK

1. Blend crushed ice in a blender with the lemon juice, sugar syrup, and chopped peach until slushy.

2. Pour into a chilled tumbler, top up with sparkling water and stir gently.

3. Decorate with raspberries and serve immediately.

INGREDIENTS

CRUSHED ICE

2 MEASURES LEMON JUICE

½ TSP SUGAR SYRUP

½ PEACH, PEELED, STONED AND CHOPPED

SPARKLING WATER

RASPBERRIES, TO DECORATE

MONTE CARLO

1. Put the ice into a mixing glass, pour over the gin and lemon juice.

2. Stir until well chilled.

3. Strain into a chilled champagne flute and top up with champagne.

4. Drizzle the crème de menthe over the top and decorate with the mint sprig.

5. Serve immediately.

SERVES 1

INGREDIENTS

4-6 ICE CUBES

½ MEASURE GIN

¼ MEASURE LEMON JUICE

CHAMPAGNE OR SPARKLING WHITE WINE, CHILLED

¼ MEASURE CRÈME DE MENTHE

FRESH MINT SPRIG, TO DECORATE

FLIRTINI

1. Put the pineapple into a mixing glass or jug.

2. Crush the pineapple and add the Cointreau, vodka and pineapple juice. Stir well.

3. Strain into a glass and top up with champagne.

4. Serve immediately.

SERVES 1

INGREDIENTS

¼ SLICE FRESH PINEAPPLE, CHOPPED

½ MEASURE CHILLED COINTREAU

½ MEASURE CHILLED VODKA

1 MEASURE CHILLED PINEAPPLE JUICE

CHILLED CHAMPAGNE

SERVES 4

PEACEMAKER

1. Put the fruit and sugar into a large punch bowl.

2. Add a little water and crush together.

3. Add the maraschino and sparkling water and mix well.

4. Top up with the champagne and decorate with the mint leaves and strawberry slices. Serve immediately.

INGREDIENTS

25 STRAWBERRIES, HULLED

½ SMALL FRESH PINEAPPLE, PEELED AND CRUSHED

1-2 TBSP ICING SUGAR

1 MEASURE MARASCHINO

225 ML/8 FL OZ SPARKLING WATER

1 BOTTLE DRY CHAMPAGNE

FRESH MINT LEAVES AND SLICED STRAWBERRIES, TO DECORATE

SERVES 1

SOUTHERN CHAMPAGNE

1. Pour the liqueur and bitters into a chilled champagne flute, and stir to mix.

2. Fill the glass with champagne. Drop the rind into the glass to decorate and serve immediately.

INGREDIENTS

1 MEASURE SOUTHERN COMFORT

DASH ANGOSTURA BITTERS

CHILLED CHAMPAGNE

TWIST OF ORANGE RIND, TO DECORATE

SERVES 1

INGREDIENTS

⅓ MEASURE AMARETTO

⅓ MEASURE DRY VERMOUTH

SPARKLING WHITE WINE

AMARETTINE

1. Mix the amaretto and vermouth in a chilled tall cocktail glass. Top up with wine to taste and serve immediately.

SERVES 1

INGREDIENTS

½ MEASURE GIN

⅛ MEASURE APRICOT BRANDY

½ MEASURE FRESH ORANGE JUICE

1 TSP GRENADINE

¼ MEASURE CINZANO

ICE

SWEET SPARKLING WINE

ORANGE AND LEMON SLICES,
TO DECORATE

SABRINA

1. Shake the first five ingredients together over ice.

2. Pour into a tall champagne flute and top up with sparkling wine.

3. Decorate with slices of orange and lemon and serve immediately.

SERVES 2

INGREDIENTS

350 ML/12 FL OZ SPARKLING WHITE WINE, REALLY COLD

2 MEASURES CRÈME DE CASSIS

1 MEASURE BRANDY

CRUSHED ICE

BLACKBERRIES, TO DECORATE

PINK SHERBET ROYALE

1. Blend half the wine in a blender with the cassis, brandy and ice until really cold and frosted.

2. Slowly whisk in a little more wine and pour into tall glasses.

3. Decorate with the blackberries and serve immediately.

KIR LETHALE

1. Put the raisin in the bottom of a chilled champagne flute.

2. Pour in the crème de cassis and vodka.

3. Fill the glass with sparkling wine and serve immediately.

SERVES 1

INGREDIENTS

1 RAISIN SOAKED IN VODKA

½ MEASURE CRÈME DE CASSIS

1 TSP VODKA

SPARKLING WINE

SERVES 1

BROKEN NEGRONI

1. Add the vermouth and bitters to a mixing glass filled with ice, and stir.

2. Strain into a chilled champagne flute.

3. Top up with sparkling wine, and decorate the glass with the orange slice. Serve immediately.

INGREDIENTS

1 MEASURE SWEET VERMOUTH

1 MEASURE CAMPARI BITTERS

ICE

SPARKLING WINE

HALF A THIN SLICE OF
ORANGE, TO DECORATE

SERVES 1

SEELBACH

1. Pour the bourbon and triple sec into a chilled champagne flute.

2. Add the bitters.

3. Top with sparkling wine.

4. Decorate the glass with the orange twist and serve immediately.

INGREDIENTS

½ MEASURE BOURBON

¼ MEASURE TRIPLE SEC

2 DASHES ANGOSTURA BITTERS

2 DASHES PEYCHAUD'S
AROMATIC BITTERS

SPARKLING WINE

ORANGE TWIST, TO DECORATE

SERVES 1

INGREDIENTS

1 MEASURE PASTIS

SPARKLING WINE

TWIST OF LEMON,
TO DECORATE

DEATH IN THE AFTERNOON

1. Pour the pastis into a chilled champagne flute.

2. Top up with sparkling wine.

3. Decorate the glass with the lemon twist and serve immediately.

SERVES 1

INGREDIENTS

1 MEASURE VODKA

½ MEASURE ORANGE-
FLAVOURED LIQUEUR

½ MEASURE FRESH LIME JUICE

1 TSP TRIPLE SEC

DASH ANGOSTURA BITTERS

CRACKED ICE

SPARKLING WINE

THE QUEEN'S COUSIN

1. Pour the vodka, orange-flavoured liqueur, fresh lime juice, triple sec and bitters into a shaker filled with ice.

2. Shake well and strain into a chilled wine glass.

3. Fill the glass with sparkling wine and serve immediately.

MIDNIGHT'S KISS

1. Spread the sugar on a plate. Run a wedge of lemon around the rim of a chilled champagne flute to moisten it, and then dip the glass in the sugar.

2. Add the vodka and curaçao to a shaker filled with ice.

3. Shake well, strain into the glass and top up with sparkling wine. Serve immediately.

SERVES 1

INGREDIENTS

SUGAR

WEDGE OF LEMON

½ MEASURE VODKA

2 TSP BLUE CURAÇAO

CRACKED ICE

SPARKLING WINE

BARTENDER'S TIP

You can use any sugar around the rim of the glass – or buy gold sugar from a specialist supplier to increase the glamour factor of this cocktail.

SERVES 1

INGREDIENTS

1 MEASURE LEMONADE

1 MEASURE CRANBERRY JUICE

ICE

SPARKLING WINE

**SPRIG OF MINT,
TO DECORATE**

PRETTY IN PINK

1. Pour the lemonade and juice into a lowball glass filled with ice.

2. Stir gently.

3. Fill the glass to the top with sparkling wine.

4. Decorate with the mint sprig and serve immediately.

INGREDIENTS

1 TBSP RAISINS
OR CHOPPED PRUNES

6 TSP BRANDY

300 ML/10 FL OZ SPARKLING
WHITE WINE OR CHAMPAGNE,
CHILLED

300 ML/10 FL OZ WHITE CRANBERRY
AND GRAPE JUICE

ICE CUBES

SAN JOAQUIN PUNCH

1. Mix the dried fruit and brandy in a small bowl and leave to soak for 1-2 hours.

2. In a jug, mix the sparkling wine, juice and brandy-soaked fruit.

3. Pour into ice-filled glasses and serve immediately.

INGREDIENTS

GRENADINE

SUGAR

½ MEASURE PEAR LIQUEUR

½ MEASURE TRIPLE SEC

2 MEASURES GRAPEFRUIT JUICE

CRACKED ICE

SPARKLING WINE

ROYAL SILVER

1. Dip the rim of a wine glass first into some grenadine and then into some sugar.

2. Pour the pear liqueur, triple sec and juice into a shaker filled with ice.

3. Shake well and strain carefully into the chilled glass.

4. Top up with sparkling wine and serve immediately.

SERVES 1

MARILYN MONROE

1. Add the brandy and grenadine to a chilled champagne glass and stir.

2. Top up with sparkling wine.

3. Hang the cherries over the edge of the glass to decorate and serve immediately.

INGREDIENTS

1 MEASURE APPLE BRANDY

1 TSP GRENADINE

SPARKLING WINE

2 COCKTAIL CHERRIES, TO DECORATE

SERVES 1

NIGHT & DAY

1. Pour the sparkling wine into a chilled champagne flute.

2. Slowly add the brandy and the orange-flavoured liqueur, then add the bitters. Serve immediately.

INGREDIENTS

3 MEASURES SPARKLING WINE

3 TSP BRANDY

2 TSP ORANGE-FLAVOURED LIQUEUR

1 TSP CAMPARI BITTERS

THE STONE FENCE

SERVES 1

INGREDIENTS

1½ MEASURES BOURBON

2 DASHES ANGOSTURA BITTERS

ICE

SPARKLING CIDER

SPRIG OF MINT, BRUISED, TO DECORATE

1. Add the bourbon and bitters to a chilled highball glass filled with ice.

2. Top up with cider.

3. Decorate with the mint sprig and serve immediately.

SERVES 1

INGREDIENTS

125 ML/4 FL OZ SPARKLING CIDER OR APPLE JUICE

1 MEASURE CALVADOS

JUICE OF ½ LEMON

1 TBSP EGG WHITE

GENEROUS PINCH SUGAR

ICE

SLICES OF LEMON AND APPLE, TO DECORATE

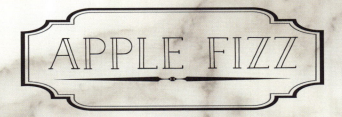

APPLE FIZZ

1. Shake the first five ingredients together over the ice.

2. Pour immediately into a glass.

3. Decorate with a slice of lemon and apple and serve immediately.

SERVES 1

APPLE BREEZE

1. Add the liqueur to a chilled highball glass half-filled with ice.

2. Top up with the cider.

3. Decorate the glass with the apple slice and serve immediately.

INGREDIENTS

1 MEASURE
COCONUT RUM

ICE

SPARKLING CIDER

SLICE OF APPLE, TO DECORATE

SERVES 4

RASPBERRY LEMONADE

1. Cut the ends off the lemons, then scoop out and chop the flesh.

2. Put the lemon flesh in a blender with the sugar, raspberries, vanilla extract and 4-6 cracked ice cubes and blend for 2-3 minutes.

3. Half fill four highball glasses with cracked ice and strain in the blended mixture.

4. Top up with sparkling water and decorate with the mint sprigs. Serve immediately.

INGREDIENTS

2 LEMONS

115 G/4 OZ ICING SUGAR

115 G/4 OZ RASPBERRIES

FEW DROPS VANILLA EXTRACT

CRACKED ICE CUBES

SPARKLING WATER

FRESH MINT SPRIGS, TO DECORATE

BLOOD ON THE TRACKS

SERVES 1

INGREDIENTS

½ MEASURE CAMPARI BITTERS

ICE

2½ MEASURES
BLOOD ORANGE JUICE

SPARKLING WATER

SLICE OF ORANGE AND
SPRIG OF MINT, TO
DECORATE

1. Pour the bitters into a chilled highball glass filled with ice.

2. Add the juice. Do not stir.

3. Top up with sparkling water.

4. Decorate with the orange slice and mint and serve immediately.

COOL COLLINS

SERVES 1

INGREDIENTS

6 FRESH MINT LEAVES, PLUS
EXTRA TO DECORATE

1 TSP CASTER SUGAR

2 MEASURES LEMON JUICE

CRACKED ICE CUBES

SPARKLING WATER

LEMON SLICE, TO DECORATE

1. Put the mint leaves into a chilled tall glass.

2. Add the sugar and lemon juice.

3. Crush the mint leaves, then stir until the sugar has dissolved.

4. Fill the glass with cracked ice cubes and top up with sparkling water.

5. Stir gently and decorate with the fresh mint and lemon slice. Serve immediately.

SERVES 1

INGREDIENTS

CRACKED ICE

2 MEASURES HAZELNUT SYRUP

2 MEASURES LEMON JUICE

1 TSP GRENADINE

SPARKLING WATER

HEAVENLY DAYS

1. Put 4-6 cracked ice cubes into a cocktail shaker.

2. Pour over the hazelnut syrup, lemon juice and grenadine and shake vigorously until well frosted.

3. Half fill a tumbler with cracked ice and strain the cocktail over.

4. Top up with sparkling water and stir gently.

5. Serve immediately.

BARTENDER'S TIP

This is the perfect alcohol-free cocktail to indulge in on a hot summer's day.

SUMMER PUNCH

1. Pour the wine into a punch bowl or large glass serving bowl. Add the honey and stir well. Add the brandy, if using.

2. Cut any large berries into bite-sized pieces and place all the berries and mint sprigs into the wine.

3. Leave to stand for 15 minutes, then add the sparkling water and ice cubes. Ladle the punch into glasses or punch cups ensuring each has an ice cube and a few pieces of fruit. Serve immediately, decorated with mint sprigs.

SERVES 8

INGREDIENTS

700 ML/1¼ PINTS ROSÉ WINE, CHILLED

1 TBSP HONEY

150 ML/5 FL OZ BRANDY
(OPTIONAL)

115 G/4 OZ MIXED SUMMER BERRIES,
SUCH AS RASPBERRIES, BLUEBERRIES
AND STRAWBERRIES

3-4 FRESH MINT SPRIGS,
PLUS EXTRA TO GARNISH

600 ML/1 PINT SPARKLING
WATER, CHILLED

ICE CUBES

SOMETHING DIFFERENT

EL DIABLO

1. Add the tequila, juice and cassis to a shaker filled with ice. Shake well.

2. Strain into a chilled highball glass filled with ice.

3. Top up with ginger ale. Decorate the glass with the lime. Serve immediately.

SERVES 1

INGREDIENTS

1 MEASURE TEQUILA

½ MEASURE FRESH LIME JUICE

½ MEASURE CRÈME DE CASSIS

CRACKED ICE

GINGER ALE

SLICE OF LIME, TO DECORATE

EL TORO

1. Pour the tequila, coffee liqueur and cream into a shaker filled with ice.

2. Shake well and strain into a chilled cocktail glass. Serve immediately.

SERVES 1

INGREDIENTS

2 MEASURES TEQUILA

1 MEASURE COFFEE LIQUEUR

1 MEASURE SINGLE CREAM

CRACKED ICE

SERVES 1

HIGH VOLTAGE

1. Pour the tequila, schnapps and juice into a shaker filled with ice.

2. Shake well and strain into a chilled cocktail glass.

3. Decorate the glass with the peach slice and serve immediately.

INGREDIENTS

2 MEASURES TEQUILA

1 MEASURE PEACH SCHNAPPS

½ MEASURE FRESH LIME JUICE

CRACKED ICE

FRESH PEACH SLICE, PEELED, TO DECORATE

SERVES 1

SILK STOCKINGS

1. Pour the tequila, liqueurs and cream into a shaker filled with ice.

2. Shake well and strain into a chilled cocktail glass.

3. Decorate the glass with raspberries on a cocktail stick. Serve immediately.

INGREDIENTS

1½ MEASURES TEQUILA

½ MEASURE RASPBERRY LIQUEUR

½ MEASURE CRÈME DE CACAO

1 MEASURE DOUBLE CREAM

CRACKED ICE

FRESH RASPBERRIES, TO DECORATE

TEQUILA SLAMMER

1. Put the tequila into a chilled glass.

2. Add the lemon juice.

3. Top up with sparkling wine.

4. Cover the glass with your hand and slam to mix.

5. Serve immediately.

SERVES 1

INGREDIENTS

1 MEASURE SILVER TEQUILA, CHILLED

JUICE OF ½ LEMON

CHILLED SPARKLING WINE

TEQUILA SUNRISE

SERVES 1

INGREDIENTS

4-6 CRACKED ICE CUBES

2 MEASURES SILVER TEQUILA

ORANGE JUICE

1 MEASURE GRENADINE

ORANGE SLICE AND COCKTAIL CHERRY, TO DECORATE

1. Put the cracked ice cubes into a chilled highball glass. Pour over the tequila.

2. Top up with orange juice.

3. Stir well to mix.

4. Slowly pour over the grenadine. Decorate with the orange slice and cocktail cherry.

5. Serve immediately.

INGREDIENTS

2 MEASURES VODKA

1 MEASURE COFFEE LIQUEUR

CRACKED ICE CUBES

BLACK RUSSIAN

1. Pour the vodka and liqueur over cracked ice cubes in a chilled lowball glass.

2. Stir to mix and serve immediately.

INGREDIENTS

1 TSP CRÈME DE MENTHE

1–2 TBSP DOUBLE CREAM

2 MEASURES COFFEE LIQUEUR OR CHOCOLATE LIQUEUR

CHOCOLATE MATCHSTICKS, TO SERVE

JEALOUSY

1. Gently beat the crème de menthe into the cream until thick.

2. Pour the coffee liqueur into a chilled shot glass and carefully spoon over the whipped flavoured cream.

3. Serve immediately with the chocolate matchsticks.

INGREDIENTS

1 MEASURE CRÈME DE
BANANE, CHILLED

**1 MEASURE IRISH CREAM
LIQUEUR, CHILLED**

BANANA SLIP

1. Pour the chilled crème de banane into a chilled shot glass.

2. With a steady hand, gently pour in the chilled cream liqueur to make a second layer. Serve immediately.

INGREDIENTS

1 MEASURE PEACH SCHNAPPS,
CHILLED

1 TSP IRISH CREAM LIQUEUR, CHILLED

½ TSP GRENADINE, CHILLED

BLOODY BRAIN

1. Pour the peach schnapps into a shot glass, then carefully pour the cream liqueur on top.

2. Finally, pour in the grenadine and serve immediately.

SERVES 1

INGREDIENTS

1 MEASURE BRANDY

1 MEASURE DRY VERMOUTH

1 MEASURE DUBONNET

CRACKED ICE

BVD

1. Pour the brandy, dry vermouth and Dubonnet over cracked ice in a mixing glass.

2. Stir to mix and strain into a chilled wine glass. Serve immediately.

BARTENDER'S TIP

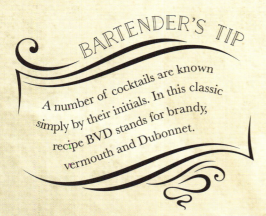

A number of cocktails are known simply by their initials. In this classic recipe BVD stands for brandy, vermouth and Dubonnet.

SERVES 1

INGREDIENTS

2 MEASURES SLOE GIN

ORANGE JUICE

CRACKED ICE CUBES

ORANGE SLICE, TO DECORATE

SLOE SCREW

1 Shake the sloe gin and orange juice over cracked ice until well frosted and pour into a chilled glass.

2 Decorate with the orange slice and serve immediately.

SERVES 1

INGREDIENTS

¾ MEASURE CRÈME DE MENTHE, CHILLED

¾ MEASURE AMARULA, CHILLED

AFRICAN MINT

1. Pour the crème de menthe into a chilled shot glass, reserving a few drops.

2. Pour the Amarula slowly over the back of a spoon to create a second layer.

3. Drizzle the remaining drops of crème de menthe over the creamy liqueur to finish. Serve immediately.

SERVES 1

INGREDIENTS

CRACKED ICE CUBES

1 MEASURE SAMBUCA

1 MEASURE ORANGE JUICE

DASH LEMON JUICE

BITTER LEMON

ZANDER

1. Fill a chilled glass with cracked ice.

2. Shake the Sambuca, orange juice and lemon juice vigorously over cracked ice until well frosted.

3. Strain into the glass and top up with bitter lemon. Serve immediately.

SERVES 1

FRENCH KISS

1. Put the cracked ice cubes into a cocktail shaker.

2. Pour over the liquid ingredients and shake vigorously until well frosted.

3. Strain into a chilled cocktail glass and serve immediately.

INGREDIENTS

4-6 CRACKED ICE CUBES

2 MEASURES BOURBON

1 MEASURE APRICOT LIQUEUR

2 TSP GRENADINE

1 TSP LEMON JUICE

SERVES 1

QUEEN OF MEMPHIS

1. Put the cracked ice cubes into a cocktail shaker.

2. Pour over the bourbon, Midori, peach juice and maraschino and shake vigorously until well frosted.

3. Strain into a chilled cocktail glass. Decorate with the melon wedge and serve immediately.

INGREDIENTS

4-6 CRACKED ICE CUBES

2 MEASURES BOURBON

1 MEASURE MIDORI

1 MEASURE PEACH JUICE

DASH MARASCHINO LIQUEUR

MELON WEDGE, TO DECORATE

RATTLESNAKE

SERVES 1

INGREDIENTS

1 MEASURE DARK CRÈME DE CACAO, CHILLED

1 MEASURE IRISH CREAM LIQUEUR, CHILLED

1 MEASURE KAHLÚA, CHILLED

1. Pour the chilled crème de cacao into a shot glass.

2. With a steady hand, gently pour in the chilled cream liqueur over the back of a spoon to make a second layer.

3. Pour in the chilled Kahlúa to make a third layer. Do not stir. Serve immediately.

BARTENDER'S TIP

This potent layered drink is named after its resemblance to the venomous snake's striped tail.

AFTER FIVE

1. Pour the peppermint schnapps into a chilled small wine glass.

2. Carefully pour the Kahlúa over the back of a spoon to make a second layer.

3. Finally, float the cream liqueur on top. Serve immediately.

SERVES 1

INGREDIENTS

½ MEASURE PEPPERMINT SCHNAPPS, CHILLED

1 MEASURE KAHLÚA, CHILLED

1 TBSP IRISH CREAM LIQUEUR

SERVES 1

INGREDIENTS

1 TSP GREEN CRÈME DE MENTHE

1 TBSP ICED WATER

1 MEASURE WHITE CRÈME DE MENTHE

2 MEASURES APPLE OR PEAR SCHNAPPS

MINTED DIAMONDS

1. Mix the green crème de menthe with the water. Pour into an ice cube tray and freeze.

2. Stir the white crème de menthe and apple or pear schnapps over ice until well frosted.

3. Strain the cocktail into a chilled cocktail glass and add the mint ice cubes. Drink when the ice cubes begin to melt.

SERVES 2

INGREDIENTS

4-6 CRACKED ICE CUBES

2 MEASURES GOLDEN RUM

1 MEASURE GALLIANO

2 MEASURES PINEAPPLE JUICE

1 MEASURE LIME JUICE

4 TSP SUGAR SYRUP

PINEAPPLE SHELL, TO SERVE

CHAMPAGNE

LIME AND LEMON SLICES AND CHERRIES, TO DECORATE

JOSIAH'S BAY FLOAT

1. Put the cracked ice cubes into a cocktail shaker.

2. Pour over the rum, Galliano, pineapple juice, lime juice and sugar syrup and shake vigorously until well frosted.

3. Strain into the pineapple shell.

4. Top up with champagne and decorate with the lime and lemon slices and cocktail cherries. Serve immediately.

SERVES 2

MELLOW MULE

1. Put the cracked ice cubes into a cocktail shaker.

2. Pour over the white rum, dark rum, golden rum, falernum and lime juice and shake vigorously until well frosted.

3. Strain the cocktail into tall, chilled tumblers.

4. Top up with ginger beer and decorate with pineapple wedges and ginger. Serve immediately.

INGREDIENTS

4-6 CRACKED ICE CUBES

2 MEASURES WHITE RUM

1 MEASURE DARK RUM

1 MEASURE GOLDEN RUM

**1 MEASURE FALERNUM
(WINE GINGER SYRUP)**

1 MEASURE LIME JUICE

GINGER BEER

PINEAPPLE WEDGES AND
GINGER, TO DECORATE

SERVES 1

BANANA DAIQUIRI

1. Put all the liquid ingredients into a blender.

2. Add the banana and blend until smooth.

3. Pour, without straining, into a chilled tumbler.

4. Decorate with the lime slice and serve immediately.

INGREDIENTS

2 MEASURES WHITE RUM,
CHILLED

½ MEASURE TRIPLE SEC, CHILLED

½ MEASURE LIME JUICE

½ MEASURE SINGLE CREAM, CHILLED

1 TSP SUGAR SYRUP

¼ BANANA, PEELED AND SLICED

LIME SLICE, TO DECORATE

CAIPIRINHA

SERVES 1

INGREDIENTS

6 LIME WEDGES

2 TSP GRANULATED SUGAR

3 MEASURES CACHAÇA

4–6 CRACKED ICE CUBES

1. Put the lime wedges in a chilled lowball glass.

2. Add the sugar.

3. Muddle the lime wedges, then pour over the cachaça.

4. Fill the glass with the cracked ice and stir well.

5. Serve immediately.

SERVES 1

INGREDIENTS

4-6 CRACKED ICE CUBES

2 MEASURES BOURBON

3 MEASURES MILK

DASH VANILLA EXTRACT

1 TSP CLEAR HONEY

FRESHLY GRATED NUTMEG,
TO DECORATE

BOURBON MILK PUNCH

1. Put the cracked ice cubes into a cocktail shaker.

2. Pour over the bourbon, milk and vanilla extract.

3. Add the honey and shake until well frosted.

4. Strain into a chilled tumbler. Sprinkle over the grated nutmeg.

5. Serve immediately.

CHERRY COLA

INGREDIENTS

6-8 ICE CUBES, CRACKED
2 MEASURES CHERRY BRANDY
1 MEASURE LEMON JUICE
COLA
LEMON SLICE

1. Half fill a chilled lowball glass with the cracked ice.

2. Pour the cherry brandy and lemon juice over the ice.

3. Top up with cola, stir gently and decorate with a slice of lemon. Serve immediately.

BLUE LAGOON

INGREDIENTS

1 MEASURE BLUE CURAÇAO
1 MEASURE VODKA
DASH LEMON JUICE
LEMONADE

1. Pour the curaçao into a chilled cocktail glass, followed by the vodka.

2. Add the lemon juice and top up with lemonade. Serve immediately.

SERVES 1

INGREDIENTS

1 MEASURE PEACH OR OTHER
SCHNAPPS, FROZEN

1 MEASURE BLACK SAMBUCA, FROZEN

TORNADO

1. Pour the schnapps into a chilled shot glass.

2. Gently pour in the sambuca over the back of a spoon.

3. Leave to stand for a few minutes to settle and separate before drinking.

SERVES 1

INGREDIENTS

¼ MEASURE PEPPERMINT SCHNAPPS

¼ MEASURE WHITE CRÈME
DE CACAO

¼ MEASURE ANISE LIQUEUR

¼ MEASURE LEMON JUICE

CRUSHED ICE

WHITE DIAMOND FRAPPÉ

1. Shake the peppermint schnapps, white crème de cacao, anise liqueur and lemon juice over some of the crushed ice until frosted.

2. Strain into a chilled lowball glass and add a small extra spoonful of crushed ice. Serve immediately.

B-52

1. Pour the crème de cacao into a shot glass.

2. With a steady hand, gently pour in the cream liqueur to make a second layer.

3. Gently pour in the Grand Marnier.

4. Cover with your hand and slam to mix, or alternatively serve with layers intact.

5. Serve immediately.

SERVES 1

INGREDIENTS

1 MEASURE CHILLED DARK CRÈME DE CACAO

1 MEASURE CHILLED IRISH CREAM LIQUEUR

1 MEASURE CHILLED GRAND MARNIER

TRICOLOUR

SERVES 1

INGREDIENTS

1 MEASURE CHILLED RED
MARASCHINO LIQUEUR

**1 MEASURE CHILLED
CRÈME DE MENTHE**

1 MEASURE CHILLED
IRISH CREAM LIQUEUR

FRESH MINT LEAF, TO DECORATE

1. Pour the maraschino into a chilled shot glass.

2. Gently pour in the crème de menthe to make a second layer.

3. Gently pour in the cream liqueur.

4. Decorate with the mint leaf.

5. Serve immediately.

SHADY LADY

1. Shake the tequila, apple brandy, cranberry juice and a dash of lime juice over ice cubes until well frosted.

2. Strain into a chilled cocktail glass and serve immediately.

INGRED ENTS

3 MEASURES TEQUILA

1 MEASURE APPLE BRANDY

1 MEASURE CRANBERRY JUICE

DASH LIME JUICE

ICE CUBES

MOO MOO

1. Pour the liqueurs and cream into a cocktail shaker filled with cracked ice.

2. Shake well and strain into a chilled highball glass filled with ice cubes.

3. Sprinkle a little cinnamon on top and serve immediately.

SERVES 1

INGREDIENTS

1 MEASURE IRISH CREAM LIQUEUR

1 MEASURE CRÈME DE CACAO

3 MEASURES SINGLE CREAM

CRACKED ICE AND ICE CUBES

GROUND CINNAMON, TO DECORATE

INGREDIENTS

1 MEASURE IRISH CREAM LIQUEUR

1 MEASURE ALMOND-FLAVOURED LIQUEUR

1 MEASURE COFFEE LIQUEUR

1 MEASURE SINGLE CREAM

CRACKED ICE AND ICE CUBES

CLIMAX

1 Pour the liqueurs and cream into a cocktail shaker filled with cracked ice.

2 Shake well and strain into a chilled lowball glass filled with ice cubes. Serve immediately.

PEACH FLOYD

1 Stir all the liquid ingredients together over cracked ice.

2 Pour into a chilled small glass and serve immediately.

SERVES 1

INGREDIENTS

1 MEASURE PEACH SCHNAPPS, CHILLED

1 MEASURE VODKA, CHILLED

1 MEASURE WHITE CRANBERRY AND PEACH JUICE, CHILLED

1 MEASURE CRANBERRY JUICE, CHILLED

CRACKED ICE CUBES

SERVES 6

INGREDIENTS

JUICE OF 1 ORANGE

JUICE OF 1 LEMON

2 TBSP ICING SUGAR

CRACKED ICE CUBES

1 ORANGE, THINLY SLICED

1 LEMON, THINLY SLICED

1 BOTTLE CHILLED RED WINE

LEMONADE, TO TASTE

SANGRIA

1. Put the orange juice and lemon juice in a large jug. Stir.

2. Add the sugar and stir. When the sugar has dissolved, add the ice cubes, sliced fruit and wine and marinate for 1 hour.

3. Add lemonade to taste, then top up with cracked ice. Serve immediately.

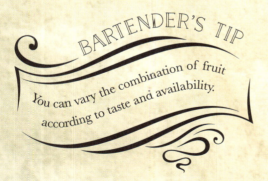

BARTENDER'S TIP

You can vary the combination of fruit according to taste and availability.

SERVES 1

INGREDIENTS

2 MEASURES DARK CRÈME DE CACAO

1 MEASURE CRÈME DE NOYAU

1 MEASURE SINGLE CREAM

CRACKED ICE

PINK SQUIRREL

1. Pour the crème de cacao, crème de noyau and single cream over the cracked ice and shake vigorously until well frosted.

2. Strain into a chilled cocktail glass and serve immediately.

SERVES 1

INGREDIENTS

1 MEASURE ABSINTHE, ICED

1 MEASURE LIME CORDIAL, ICED

CRACKED ICE CUBES

FIRELIGHTER

1. Shake the absinthe and lime cordial vigorously over cracked ice until well frosted.

2. Strain into a chilled shot glass and serve immediately.

SERVES 1

INGREDIENTS

1½ MEASURES AMARETTO

SUGAR

FRESHLY MADE STRONG
BLACK COFFEE

1–2 TBSP DOUBLE CREAM

AMARETTO COFFEE

1. Put the amaretto into a warmed heatproof glass and add sugar to taste.

2. Pour in the coffee and stir.

3. When the sugar has completely dissolved, pour in the cream very slowly over the back of a spoon so that it floats on top.

4. Don't stir - drink the coffee through the cream.

SERVES 1

AMARETTO STINGER

1. Shake the amaretto and white crème de menthe vigorously over cracked ice until well frosted.

2. Strain into a chilled lowball glass and serve immediately.

INGREDIENTS

2 MEASURES AMARETTO

1 MEASURE WHITE CRÈME DE MENTHE

CRACKED ICE CUBES

SERVES 1

MUDSLIDE

1. Shake the Kahlúa, cream liqueur and vodka vigorously over cracked ice until well frosted.

2. Strain into a chilled glass and serve immediately.

INGREDIENTS

1½ MEASURES KAHLÚA

1½ MEASURES IRISH CREAM LIQUEUR

1½ MEASURES VODKA

CRACKED ICE CUBES

SERVES 1

INGREDIENTS

1 MEASURE IRISH CREAM
LIQUEUR

**1 MEASURE WHITE CRÈME
DE MENTHE**

CRACKED ICE CUBES

IRISH STINGER

1. Shake the cream liqueur and white crème de menthe vigorously over cracked ice until well frosted.

2. Strain into a chilled shot or lowball glass.

BARTENDER'S TIP

Substitute the Irish cream liqueur for 2 measures of brandy to make the classic Stinger cocktail instead.

WHITE COSMOPOLITAN

1. Shake the limoncello, Cointreau and white cranberry and grape juice over cracked ice until frosted.

2. Strain into a chilled glass.

3. Add the bitters and decorate with the cranberries and serve immediately.

SERVES 1

INGREDIENTS

1½ MEASURES LIMONCELLO

½ MEASURE COINTREAU

1 MEASURE WHITE CRANBERRY AND GRAPE JUICE

CRACKED ICE CUBES

DASH ORANGE BITTERS

CRANBERRIES, TO DECORATE

CHOCOLATE MARTINI

SERVES 1

1. Moisten the rim of a cocktail glass with an orange slice. Dip in cocoa powder and set aside.

2. Shake the vodka, crème de cacao and orange flower water over ice cubes until really well frosted.

3. Strain into the cocktail glass and decorate with a twist of orange peel. Serve immediately.

INGREDIENTS

SLICE OF ORANGE

COCOA POWDER

2 MEASURES VODKA

¼ MEASURE CRÈME DE CACAO

2 DASHES ORANGE FLOWER WATER

ICE CUBES

TWIST OF ORANGE PEEL

ALABAMA SLAMMER

SERVES 1

1. Pour the Southern Comfort, amaretto and sloe gin over cracked ice in a mixing glass and stir.

2. Strain into a shot glass and add the lemon juice. Cover with your hand, slam on the table and drink immediately.

INGREDIENTS

1 MEASURE SOUTHERN COMFORT

1 MEASURE AMARETTO

1 MEASURE SLOE GIN

CRACKED ICE

½ TSP LEMON JUICE

SERVES 1

INGREDIENTS

CRUSHED ICE

2 MEASURES DRAMBUIE

1 MEASURE TOFFEE LIQUEUR,
ICED

TOFFEE SPLIT

1. Fill a shot glass with crushed ice.

2. Pour the Drambuie over the ice, then pour in the toffee liqueur over the back of a spoon to make a layer on top. Serve immediately.

SERVES 1

INGREDIENTS

½ MEASURE KAHLÚA

½ MEASURE MALIBU, CHILLED

½ MEASURE BUTTERSCOTCH
SCHNAPPS, CHILLED

1 MEASURE MILK, CHILLED

VOODOO

1. Pour the Kahlúa, Malibu, butterscotch schnapps and milk into a chilled shot glass.

2. Stir well. Serve immediately.

SERVES 1

INGREDIENTS

1¼ MEASURES COGNAC

1 MEASURE DARK CRÈME DE CACAO

¼ MEASURE CRÈME DE BANANE

CRACKED ICE CUBES

1 TBSP CREAM

NAPOLEON'S NIGHTCAP

1. Stir the cognac, crème de cacao and crème de banane in a mixing glass with cracked ice.

2. Strain into a chilled cocktail glass and float the cream on top. Serve immediately.

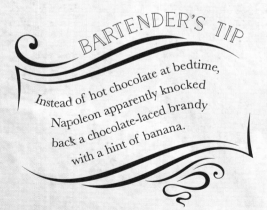

BARTENDER'S TIP

Instead of hot chocolate at bedtime, Napoleon apparently knocked back a chocolate-laced brandy with a hint of banana.

IRISH COFFEE

1. Put the whiskey into a warmed heatproof glass and add sugar to taste.

2. Pour in the coffee and stir.

3. When the sugar has completely dissolved, pour in the cream very slowly over the back of a spoon so that it floats on top.

4. Don't stir - drink the coffee through the cream.

SERVES 1

INGREDIENTS

2 MEASURES IRISH WHISKEY

SUGAR

FRESHLY MADE STRONG BLACK COFFEE

2 MEASURES DOUBLE CREAM

MOCKTAILS

SERVES 1

INGREDIENTS

CRACKED ICE CUBES

6 MEASURES MILK

3 MEASURES COCONUT CREAM

4 MEASURES PINEAPPLE JUICE

TO DECORATE

PINEAPPLE CHUNK

PINEAPPLE LEAF

COCKTAIL CHERRY

MINI COLADA

1. Put 4-6 cracked ice cubes into a cocktail shaker.

2. Pour over the milk and coconut cream.

3. Add the pineapple juice and shake vigorously until well frosted.

4. Half fill a highball glass with cracked ice, strain the cocktail into it and decorate with the pineapple chunk, pineapple leaf and cherry. Serve immediately.

SERVES 1

INGREDIENTS

CRACKED ICE CUBES

2 MEASURES LEMON JUICE

½ MEASURE GRENADINE

½ MEASURE SUGAR SYRUP

GINGER ALE

ORANGE SLICE, TO DECORATE

SHIRLEY TEMPLE

1. Put 4-6 cracked ice cubes into a cocktail shaker.

2. Pour over the lemon juice, grenadine and sugar syrup and shake vigorously until well frosted.

3. Half fill a chilled highball glass with cracked ice, then strain the cocktail over it.

4. Top up with ginger ale and decorate with the orange slice. Serve immediately.

INGREDIENTS

CRACKED ICE CUBES

3 MEASURES PINEAPPLE JUICE

2 MEASURES LIME JUICE

1 MEASURE GREEN PEPPERMINT SYRUP

GINGER ALE

CUCUMBER STRIP AND LIME SLICE, TO DECORATE

BRIGHT GREEN COOLER

1. Put 4-6 cracked ice cubes into a cocktail shaker.

2. Pour over the pineapple juice, lime juice and peppermint syrup and shake vigorously until well frosted.

3. Half fill a chilled highball glass with cracked ice and strain the cocktail over it.

4. Top up with ginger ale and decorate with the cucumber strip and lime slice. Serve immediately.

INGREDIENTS

175 ML/6 FL OZ ORANGE JUICE

175 ML/6 FL OZ SPARKLING WHITE GRAPE JUICE

ORANGE SLICES, TO DECORATE

MAIDENLY MIMOSA

1. Chill two champagne flutes.

2. Divide the orange juice between the flutes and top up with the sparkling grape juice.

3. Decorate with the orange slices and serve immediately.

SERVES 6

INGREDIENTS

350 ML/1½ PINTS APPLE JUICE

350 ML/12 FL OZ
LEMON JUICE

125 ML/4 FL OZ
SUGAR SYRUP

CRACKED ICE CUBES

**2.25 LITRES/4 PINTS
GINGER ALE**

ORANGE SLICES,
TO DECORATE

BARTENDER'S TIP

This is the perfect punch to serve to children at a summer party.

PROHIBITION PUNCH

1. Pour the apple juice into a large jug.

2. Add the lemon juice and sugar syrup and a handful of cracked ice cubes.

3. Add the ginger ale and stir gently to mix. Pour into chilled lowball glasses and decorate with the orange slices. Serve immediately.

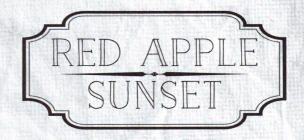

RED APPLE SUNSET

1. Shake the apple juice, grapefruit juice and a dash of grenadine over ice cubes until well frosted.

2. Strain into a chilled cocktail glass and serve immediately.

SERVES 1

INGREDIENTS

2 MEASURES APPLE JUICE

2 MEASURES GRAPEFRUIT JUICE

DASH GRENADINE

ICE CUBES

SERVES 1

INGREDIENTS

4-6 CRACKED ICE CUBES

**1½ MEASURES
RASPBERRY SYRUP**

CHILLED SPARKLING APPLE
JUICE

FAUX KIR ROYALE

1 Put the cracked ice cubes into a mixing glass. Pour over the raspberry syrup.

2 Stir well to mix and strain into a chilled wine glass.

3 Top up with sparkling apple juice and stir. Serve immediately.

SERVES 1

INGREDIENTS

1 MEASURE LIME JUICE

1 MEASURE BARBECUE SAUCE

WORCESTERSHIRE SAUCE

HOT PEPPER SAUCE

ICE CUBES

TOMATO JUICE

LIME SLICES AND
1 PICKLED JALAPEÑO CHILLI
TO DECORATE

RANCH GIRL

1 Shake the lime juice, barbecue sauce and dashes of Worcestershire sauce and hot pepper sauce over ice cubes until well frosted.

2 Pour into a chilled highball glass, top up with tomato juice and stir.

3 Decorate with a couple of slices of lime and a pickled jalapeño chilli. Serve immediately.

SERVES 1

INGREDIENTS

2 MEASURES PEACH JUICE

1 MEASURE LEMON JUICE

SPARKLING APPLE JUICE

BABY BELLINI

1. Pour the peach juice and lemon juice into a chilled champagne flute and stir well.

2. Top up with sparkling apple juice and stir again. Serve immediately.

SERVES 1

INGREDIENTS

CRUSHED ICE

5 MEASURES APPLE JUICE

1 MEASURE LIME JUICE

½ TSP ORGEAT SYRUP

1 TBSP APPLE SAUCE OR APPLE PURÉE

GROUND CINNAMON

BITE OF THE APPLE

1. Whizz the crushed ice in a blender with the apple juice, lime juice, orgeat syrup and apple sauce until smooth.

2. Pour into a chilled lowball glass and sprinkle with cinnamon. Serve immediately.

SERVES 1

INGREDIENTS

4-5 CRACKED ICE CUBES

2 MEASURES TOMATO JUICE

1 MEASURE LEMON JUICE

2 DASHES WORCESTERSHIRE SAUCE

1 DASH HOT PEPPER SAUCE

PINCH CELERY SALT

PEPPER

LEMON WEDGE AND CELERY STICK, TO DECORATE

VIRGIN MARY

1. Put the cracked ice cubes into a cocktail shaker. Pour over the tomato juice.

2. Add the lemon juice.

3. Pour in the Worcestershire sauce and hot pepper sauce. Shake vigorously until well frosted.

4. Season to taste with the celery salt and pepper, strain into a chilled glass and decorate with the lemon wedge and celery stick.

5. Serve immediately.

SERVES 6

INGREDIENTS

475 ML/16 FL OZ TOMATO JUICE

225 ML/3 FL OZ ORANGE JUICE

3 MEASURES LIME JUICE

½ MEASURE HOT PEPPER SAUCE

2 TSP WORCESTERSHIRE SAUCE

1 JALAPEÑO CHILLI, DESEEDED AND FINELY CHOPPED

CELERY SALT

WHITE PEPPER (PREFERABLY FRESHLY GROUND)

CRACKED ICE

SANGRÍA SECA

1. Pour the tomato, orange and lime juice and the hot pepper and Worcestershire sauce into a jug.

2. Add the chilli and season with the celery salt and white pepper.

3. Stir well and chill in the refrigerator for at least an hour.

4. To serve, half fill chilled highball glasses with cracked ice and strain the cocktail over it.

5. Serve immediately.

SERVES 1

INGREDIENTS

CRACKED ICE

2 MEASURES APRICOT JUICE

RASPBERRY JUICE

ORANGE PEEL TWIST AND
A FEW RASPBERRIES, TO
DECORATE

KNICKS VICTORY COOLER

1. Half fill a chilled highball glass with the cracked ice.

2. Pour the apricot juice over the ice, top up with raspberry juice and stir gently.

3. Decorate with an orange peel twist and fresh raspberries. Serve immediately.

SERVES 2

INGREDIENTS

CRUSHED ICE

DASH HOT PEPPER SAUCE

DASH WORCESTERSHIRE SAUCE

1 TSP LEMON JUICE

1 CARROT, CHOPPED

2 CELERY STICKS, CHOPPED

300 ML/10 FL OZ TOMATO JUICE

150 ML/5 FL OZ CLAM JUICE

SALT AND FRESHLY GROUND
BLACK PEPPER

**CELERY STICKS, TO
DECORATE**

NEW ENGLAND PARTY

1. Put all the ingredients, except the seasoning and celery stick, into a blender and blend until smooth.

2. Transfer to a jug, cover and chill in the refrigerator for about an hour.

3. Pour into two chilled highball glasses and season to taste.

4. Decorate with a celery stick and serve immediately.

SERVES 2

FRUIT COOLER

1. Pour the orange juice and yogurt into a food processor and process gently until combined.

2. Add the eggs and frozen bananas and process until smooth.

3. Pour the mixture into highball or hurricane glasses and decorate the rims with slices of fresh banana. Serve immediately.

INGREDIENTS

225 ML/8 FL OZ ORANGE JUICE

125 ML/4 FL OZ NATURAL YOGURT

2 EGGS

2 BANANAS, SLICED AND FROZEN

FRESH BANANA SLICES

SERVES 1

CITRUS FIZZ

1. Rub the rim of a champagne flute with orange or lime juice and dip into the icing sugar.

2. Stir the rest of the juices together with the bitters and then pour into the glass.

3. Add sparkling water to taste and serve immediately.

INGREDIENTS

2 MEASURES FRESH ORANGE JUICE, CHILLED

ICING SUGAR

SQUEEZE LIME JUICE

FEW DROPS ANGOSTURA BITTERS

2–3 MEASURES SPARKLING WATER, CHILLED

MANGO LASSI

SERVES 2

INGREDIENTS

225 ML/8 FL OZ MILK

125 ML/4 FL OZ NATURAL YOGURT

1 TBSP ROSE WATER

3 TBSP HONEY

1 RIPE MANGO, PEELED AND DICED

4–6 ICE CUBES

ROSE PETALS, TO DECORATE (OPTIONAL)

1. Pour the milk and yogurt into a blender and process until combined.

2. Add the rose water and honey and process until blended.

3. Add the mango and ice cubes and blend until smooth.

4. Pour into two chilled glasses and decorate with the rose petals, if using.

5. Serve immediately.

COCONUT CREAM

1. Pour the pineapple juice and coconut milk into a blender.

2. Add the ice cream and process until smooth.

3. Add the pineapple chunks and process until smooth.

4. Divide between two chilled glasses and decorate with the grated coconut.

5. Serve immediately.

SERVES 2

INGREDIENTS

350 ML/12 FL OZ PINEAPPLE JUICE

90 ML/3 FL OZ COCONUT MILK

150 G/5½ OZ VANILLA ICE CREAM

140 G/5 OZ FROZEN PINEAPPLE CHUNKS

GRATED FRESH COCONUT, TO DECORATE

SERVES 1

COCOBERRY

1. Rub the raspberries through a sieve with the back of a spoon and transfer the purée to a blender.

2. Add the crushed ice, coconut cream and pineapple juice and blend until smooth, then pour the mixture, without straining, into a chilled lowball glass.

3. Decorate with a pineapple wedge and fresh raspberries. Serve immediately.

INGREDIENTS

90 G/3¼ OZ RASPBERRIES

CRUSHED ICE

1 MEASURE COCONUT CREAM

150 ML/5 FL OZ PINEAPPLE JUICE

PINEAPPLE WEDGE

A FEW RASPBERRIES

SERVES 1

COCOBELLE

1. Blend the first four ingredients in a blender until slushy.

2. Chill a tall glass and gently dribble a few splashes of grenadine down the insides.

3. Pour in the slush slowly and top with the toasted coconut. Serve immediately.

INGREDIENTS

3 MEASURES COLD MILK

1 MEASURE COCONUT CREAM

2 SCOOPS VANILLA ICE CREAM

3–4 ICE CUBES

DASH GRENADINE

DESICCATED COCONUT, TOASTED, TO DECORATE

SERVES 1

SLUSH PUPPY

1. Pour the lemon juice and grenadine into a chilled tall glass with ice.

2. Add the lemon peel, syrup and soda water to taste. Decorate with a cherry and serve immediately.

INGREDIENTS

JUICE OF 1 LEMON OR ½ PINK GRAPEFRUIT

2 TBSP GRENADINE

ICE CUBES

FEW STRIPS OF LEMON PEEL

2-3 TSP RASPBERRY SYRUP

SODA WATER

COCKTAIL CHERRY, TO DECORATE

SERVES 1

THAI FRUIT COCKTAIL

1. Shake the ingredients over ice in a cocktail shaker.

2. Pour into a chilled long glass and finish with a flower. Serve immediately.

INGREDIENTS

50 ML/2 FL OZ PINEAPPLE JUICE

50 ML/2 FL OZ ORANGE JUICE

1 TBSP LIME JUICE

50 ML/2 FL OZ PASSION FRUIT JUICE

100 ML/3½ FL OZ GUAVA JUICE

CRUSHED ICE

FLOWER, TO DECORATE

SERVES 1

INGREDIENTS

4-6 CRACKED ICE CUBES

4 MEASURES APPLE JUICE

1 SMALL SCOOP VANILLA
ICE CREAM

SODA WATER

**CINNAMON SUGAR AND
APPLE, TO DECORATE**

APPLE PIE CREAM

1. Put the cracked ice cubes into a blender and add the apple juice and ice cream.

2. Blend for 10-15 seconds until frothy and frosted. Pour into a glass and top up with soda water.

3. Sprinkle over the cinnamon sugar and decorate with an apple slice. Serve immediately.

BARTENDER'S TIP

For an alcoholic version of this sweet treat, use apple cider instead of the apple juice.

PEACHY CREAM

1. Pour the peach juice and cream together over ice cubes and shake vigorously until well frosted.

2. Half fill a chilled highball glass or lowball glass with cracked ice and strain the cocktail over it. Serve immediately.

SERVES 1

INGREDIENTS

2 MEASURES PEACH JUICE, CHILLED

2 MEASURES SINGLE CREAM

CRACKED ICE

GINGER FIZZ

1. Put 2 measures of ginger ale into a blender, add a few mint sprigs and blend together.

2. Strain into a chilled highball glass two-thirds filled with cracked ice and top up with more ginger ale.

3. Decorate with raspberries and the mint sprig. Serve immediately.

INGREDIENTS

GINGER ALE

FRESH MINT SPRIGS, PLUS EXTRA TO DECORATE

CRACKED ICE

FRESH RASPBERRIES, TO DECORATE

SERVES 1

SOBER SUNDAY

1. Pour the grenadine and fruit juice into an ice-filled highball glass.

2. Top up with lemonade and finish with slices of lemon and lime. Serve immediately.

INGREDIENTS

50 ML/2 FL OZ GRENADINE

50 ML/2 FL OZ FRESH LEMON OR LIME JUICE

ICE CUBES

LEMONADE

FRESH LEMON OR LIME SLICES, TO DECORATE

SERVES 1

INGREDIENTS

ICE CUBES

1 MEASURE LIME CORDIAL

GINGER BEER

LIME WEDGE AND MINT SPRIG,
TO DECORATE

LONG BOAT

1. Fill a chilled glass two-thirds full with the ice and pour in the lime cordial.

2. Top up with ginger beer and stir gently.

3. Decorate with the lime wedge and the mint sprig. Serve immediately.

SERVES 2

INGREDIENTS

300 ML/10 FL OZ CRANBERRY
JUICE

125 ML/4 FL OZ ORANGE JUICE

55 G/2 OZ FRESH
RASPBERRIES

1 TBSP LEMON JUICE

**FRESH ORANGE SLICES,
TO DECORATE**

CRANBERRY ENERGIZER

1. Pour the cranberry juice and orange juice into a blender and blend gently until combined.

2. Add the raspberries and lemon juice and blend until smooth.

3. Strain into glasses and decorate with the slices of orange. Serve immediately.

THE GUNNER

1. Mix all the ingredients together in a long glass.

2. Taste and add more Angostura bitters if you wish. Serve immediately.

SERVES 1

INGREDIENTS

4-6 ICE CUBES

50 ML/2 FL OZ LIME JUICE

2-3 DASHES ANGOSTURA BITTERS, OR TO TASTE

200 ML/7 FL OZ GINGER BEER

200 ML/7 FL OZ LEMONADE

BARTENDER'S TIP

The Gunner is renowned for being light and refreshing, perfect for a hot summer evening.

PEAR & RASPBERRY DELIGHT

1. Put the pears into a blender with the raspberries and water and blend until smooth.

2. Taste and sweeten with honey if the raspberries are a little sharp.

3. Strain into glasses and decorate with the raspberries. Serve immediately.

SERVES 2

INGREDIENTS

2 LARGE RIPE ANJOU PEARS, PEELED, CORED AND CHOPPED

140 G/5 OZ FROZEN RASPBERRIES

175 ML/6 FL OZ ICE-COLD WATER

HONEY, TO TASTE

RASPBERRIES, TO DECORATE

STRAWBERRY COLADA

1. Reserve four strawberries to decorate. Halve the remainder and place in the blender.

2. Add the coconut cream and pineapple juice and blend until smooth, then pour into chilled glasses and decorate with the reserved strawberries. Serve immediately.

INGREDIENTS

450 G/1 LB STRAWBERRIES

125 ML/4 FL OZ COCONUT CREAM

600 ML/1 PINT CHILLED PINEAPPLE JUICE

ST. CLEMENTS

1. Put the ice cubes into a chilled tumbler. Pour in the orange juice and bitter lemon.

2. Stir gently and decorate with the slices of orange and lemon. Serve immediately.

INGREDIENTS

ICE CUBES

2 MEASURES ORANGE JUICE

2 MEASURES BITTER LEMON

ORANGE AND LEMON SLICES, TO DECORATE

SERVES 2

INGREDIENTS

300 ML/10 FL OZ MILK

4 TBSP INSTANT COFFEE POWDER

140 G/5 OZ VANILLA ICE CREAM

2 BANANAS, SLICED AND FROZEN, PLUS EXTRA SLICES TO DECORATE

BROWN SUGAR, TO TASTE

BANANA COFFEE BREAK

1. Pour the milk into a food processor, add the coffee powder and process gently until combined. Add half the vanilla ice cream and process gently, then add the remaining ice cream and process until well combined.

2. When thoroughly blended, add the bananas and sugar to taste and process until smooth.

3. Pour into chilled glasses and serve, decorated with a few slices of banana. Serve immediately.

SERVES 1

INGREDIENTS

4 MEASURES PINEAPPLE JUICE

2 MEASURES COCONUT CREAM

CUP OF CRUSHED ICE

PINEAPPLE CHUNK AND COCKTAIL CHERRY, TO DECORATE

COCO COLADA

1. Pour the juice and coconut cream into a blender, and add the ice.

2. Blend until combined and slushy and pour into a chilled glass.

3. Decorate the glass with the pineapple and cocktail cherry on a stick. Serve immediately.

INGREDIENTS

1.5 LITRES/2½ PINTS RED GRAPE JUICE

300 ML/10 FL OZ ORANGE JUICE

75 ML/2½ FL OZ CRANBERRY JUICE

50 ML/2 FL OZ LEMON JUICE

50 ML/2 FL OZ LIME JUICE

100 ML/3½ FL OZ SUGAR SYRUP

ICE CUBES

LEMON, ORANGE AND LIME SLICES, TO DECORATE

BARTENDER'S TIP

This is a non-alcoholic version of the Spanish classic. Make sure all ingredients are well chilled before combining.

SOFT SANGRIA

1. Put the grape juice, orange juice, cranberry juice, lemon juice, lime juice and sugar syrup into a chilled punch bowl and stir well.

2. Add the ice and decorate with the slices of lemon, orange and lime.

SERVES 1

INGREDIENTS

CRACKED ICE

2 MEASURES ORANGE JUICE

1 MEASURE LEMON JUICE

1 MEASURE GRENADINE

SPARKLING MINERAL WATER

SUNRISE

1. Put the cracked ice into a chilled highball glass and pour the orange juice, lemon juice and grenadine over it.

2. Stir together well and top up with sparkling mineral water. Serve immediately.

SERVES 1

INGREDIENTS

JUICE OF ½ LEMON

1 EGG WHITE

1 DASH GRENADINE

CRUSHED ICE

LEMONADE

LEMON SLICE,
TO DECORATE

POM POM

1. Shake the lemon juice, egg white and grenadine together and strain over crushed ice in a tall glass.

2. Top up with lemonade and decorate with a lemon slice on the rim of the glass. Serve immediately.

SERVES 4

INGREDIENTS

CRACKED ICE

2 BANANAS

225 ML/3 FL OZ PINEAPPLE JUICE, CHILLED

125 ML/4 FL OZ LIME JUICE

PINEAPPLE SLICES, TO DECORATE

PERKY PINEAPPLE

1. Put the cracked ice into a blender. Peel the bananas and slice directly into the blender. Add the pineapple and lime juice and blend until smooth.

2. Pour into chilled glasses and decorate with the slices of pineapple. Serve immediately.

SERVES 1

MOCHA SLUSH

1. Whizz the crushed ice in a small blender with the coffee and chocolate syrups and milk until slushy.

2. Pour into a chilled glass and sprinkle with grated chocolate. Serve immediately.

INGREDIENTS

CRUSHED ICE CUBES

100 ML/3½ FL OZ COFFEE SYRUP

3 TBSP CHOCOLATE SYRUP

200 ML/7 FL OZ MILK

GRATED CHOCOLATE

SERVES 2

MOCHA CREAM

1. Put the milk, cream and sugar into a food processor or blender and process gently until combined.

2. Add the cocoa powder and coffee syrup and process well, then add the ice cubes and process until smooth.

3. Pour the mixture into glasses. Top with whipped cream, scatter the grated chocolate over the drinks and serve immediately.

INGREDIENTS

200 ML/7 FL OZ MILK

50 ML/2 FL OZ SINGLE CREAM

1 TBSP BROWN SUGAR

2 TBSP COCOA POWDER

1 TBSP COFFEE SYRUP OR INSTANT COFFEE POWDER

6 ICE CUBES

WHIPPED CREAM AND GRATED CHOCOLATE, TO DECORATE

SERVES 1

INGREDIENTS

ICE CUBES

3 MEASURES LEMONADE

3 MEASURES ICED TEA

ARNOLD PALMER

1. Half fill a chilled highball glass with ice cubes and pour in the lemonade.

2. Slowly pour in the tea, so that it does not mix.

3. Serve immediately with a straw.

BARTENDER'S TIP

This refreshing combination of iced tea and lemonade is named after American golfer Arnold Palmer.

SALTY PUPPY

1. Mix equal quantities of the sugar and salt together on a saucer.

2. Rub the rim of a chilled highball glass with a wedge of lime and dip it into the sugar and salt mixture to frost.

3. Fill the glass with cracked ice and pour the lime juice over them. Top up with grapefruit juice and serve immediately.

SERVES 1

INGREDIENTS

GRANULATED SUGAR

COARSE SALT

WEDGE OF LIME

CRACKED ICE

½ MEASURE LIME JUICE

GRAPEFRUIT JUICE

SERVES 1

INGREDIENTS

10-12 ICE CUBES

HOT PEPPER SAUCE

WORCESTERSHIRE SAUCE

4 MEASURES TOMATO JUICE

4 MEASURES CLAM JUICE

¼ TSP HORSERADISH SAUCE

CELERY SALT AND PEPPER

CELERY STICK AND LIME, TO DECORATE

CLAM DIGGER

1. Put 4-6 ice cubes into a cocktail shaker. Dash the hot pepper and Worcestershire sauce over the ice, pour in the tomato juice and clam juice and add the horseradish sauce. Shake vigorously until frosted.

2. Fill a chilled highball glass with cracked ice cubes and strain the cocktail over them. Season to taste with celery salt and pepper and decorate with a celery stick and lime wedge. Serve immediately.

SERVES 4

INGREDIENTS

1 PINEAPPLE

4 MEASURES PINEAPPLE JUICE

2 TBSP CREAMED COCONUT

4 MEASURES MILK

2 TBSP CRUSHED PINEAPPLE

3 TBSP COCONUT FLAKES

CRUSHED ICE

CHERRIES AND PINEAPPLE LEAVES, TO DECORATE

COCONUT ISLANDER

1. Cut the top off the pineapple and remove the flesh. Use some of the flesh and set aside the rest for a salad or dessert.

2. Whizz all the liquid ingredients in a blender with the coconut flakes and a little crushed ice for 30-40 seconds.

3. When smooth and frothy, pour into the pineapple shell, decorate with cherries or the pineapple leaves and serve immediately with straws.

SERVES 10

INGREDIENTS

600 ML/1 PINT CRANBERRY JUICE

600 ML/1 PINT ORANGE JUICE

150 ML/5 FL OZ WATER

½ TSP GROUND GINGER

¼ TSP CINNAMON

¼ TSP GRATED NUTMEG

CRACKED ICE

CRANBERRIES, TO DECORATE

CRANBERRY PUNCH

1. Put the first six ingredients into a saucepan and bring to the boil. Reduce the heat to low and simmer for 5 minutes.

2. Remove from the heat and pour into a heatproof jug or bowl. Chill in the refrigerator.

3. Remove from the refrigerator, put cracked ice into the serving glasses, pour in the punch, and decorate with cranberries on cocktail sticks.

SERVES 6

INGREDIENTS

600 ML/1 PINT LEMONADE, CHILLED

450 ML/16 FL OZ COLA, CHILLED

450 ML/16 FL OZ DRY GINGER ALE, CHILLED

JUICE OF 1 ORANGE

JUICE OF 1 LEMON

FEW DROPS ANGOSTURA BITTERS

SLICED FRUIT AND MINT SPRIGS

ICE CUBES

NON-ALCOHOLIC PIMM'S

1. Mix the first six ingredients together thoroughly in a large jug or punch bowl.

2. Float in the fruit and mint, keep in a cold place and add the ice cubes just before serving.

A Sloe Kiss 21
absinthe: Firelighter 148
African Mint 132
After Five 135
Alabama Slammer 152
Alaska 26
amaretto
  A Sloe Kiss 21
  Alabama Slammer 152
  Amarettine 107
  Amaretto Coffee 148
  Amaretto Stinger 149
  Goddaughter 85
  Ocean Breeze 61
Amarula
  African Mint 132
  Vodka Espresso 53
Apple Breeze 118
Apple Fizz 117
Apple Pie Cream 172
Arnold Palmer 184
Aurora Borealis 46

B-52 142
Baby Bellini 163
Bachelor's Bait 35
Bajan Sun 60
Banana Coffee Break 179
Banana Colada 56
Banana Daiquiri 137
Banana Slip 129
Beadlestone 76
Beagle 85
Belle Collins 19
Bellini 96
Bite of the Apple 163
Black Beauty 42
Black Russian 128
Black Velvet 101
Bleu Bleu Bleu 31
Blood On The Tracks 119
Bloodhound 25
Bloody Brain 129
Bloody Caesar 44
Bloody Mary 44
Blue Blooded 30
Blue Hawaiian 61
Blue Lagoon 140
Blue Monday 43
Boston Sour 71
Bourbon Milk Punch 139
brandy
  Bajan Sun 60
  Beagle 85
  Brandy Alexander 86
  Brandy Julep 81
  Brandy Sour 80
  BVD 130
  Champagne Cocktail 92
  Champagne
    Pick-Me-Up 93
  Cherry Cola 140
  Cherry Kitsch 84
  Cuban 80
  First Night 83
  Goddaughter 85
  Heavenly 84
  Hot Brandy Chocolate 87
  Kir Royale 90
  Kismet 95
  Marilyn Monroe 115
  Midnight Cowboy 79
  Napoleon's Nightcap 154
  Night & Day 115
  Peartini 41
  Pink Sherbet Royale 108
  Pink Whiskers 82
  Sabrina 107
  San Joaquin Punch 114
  Shady Lady 144
  Sidecar 81
  Singapore Sling 18
  Summer Punch 121

The Bentley 99
The Reviver 78
Wedding Belle 27
Bride's Mother 27
Bright Green Cooler 159
Broken Negroni 110
Buck's Fizz 94
BVD 130

Caipirinha 138
Caribbean Champagne 102
champagne
  Bellini 96
  Buck's Fizz 94
  Caribbean
    Champagne 102
  Champagne Cocktail 92
  Champagne
    Pick-Me-Up 93
  Champagne Sidecar 91
  Diamond Fizz 91
  Duke 94
  Flirtini 105
  Jade 103
  Josiah's Bay Float 136
  Kir Royale 90
  Kismet 95
  London French 75 95
  Mimosa 97
  Monte Carlo 104
  Peacemaker 106
  Royal Julep 102
  San Joaquin Punch 114
  San Remo 98
  Southern Champagne 106
  Sparkling Gold 98
  The Bentley 99
  Wild Silk 100
Chartreuse
  Alaska 26
  Aurora Borealis 46
  Green Lady 34
  Shamrock 72
Cherry Cola 140
Cherry Kitsch 84
Chocolate Martini 152
cider
  Apple Breeze 118
  Apple Fizz 117
  The Stone Fence 116
Citrus Fizz 167
Clam Digger 186
Climax 145
Club Mojito 59
Coco Colada 179
Cocobelle 170
Cocoberry 170
Coconut Cream 169
Coconut Islander 186
coffee liqueur
  Black Russian 128
  Climax 145
  El Toro 124
  First Night 83
  Jealousy 128
  Midnight Cowboy 79
Cointreau
  Blue Monday 43
  Champagne Sidecar 91
  Flirtini 105
  Sparkling Gold 98
  White Cosmopolitan 151
Colleen 77
Cool Collins 119
Cordless Screwdriver 43
Cosmopolitan 36
Cranberry Collins 50
Cranberry Energizer 175
Cranberry Punch 187
crème de banane
  Banana Slip 129
  Caribbean
    Champagne 102

Disco Dancer 90
Napoleon's Nightcap 154
crème de cacao
  B-52 142
  Brandy Alexander 86
  Chocolate Martini 152
  Flying Grasshopper 46
  Moo Moo 144
  Napoleon's Nightcap 154
  Pink Squirrel 147
  Rattlesnake 134
  Silk Stockings 125
  White Diamond
    Frappé 141
crème de cassis
  Aurora Borealis 46
  El Diablo 124
  Kir Lethale 109
  Kir Royale 90
crème de menthe
  African Mint 132
  Amaretto Stinger 149
  Flying Grasshopper 46
  Irish Stinger 150
  Jealousy 128
  Long Island Iced Tea 45
  Minted Diamonds 136
  Monte Carlo 104
  Shamrock 72
  The Reviver 78
  Tricolour 143
Creole Lady 35
Cuba Libre 64
Cuban 80
Cuban Special 64
curaçao
  Aurora Borealis 46
  Bleu Bleu Bleu 31
  Blue Blooded 30
  Blue Hawaiian 61
  Blue Lagoon 140
  Blue Monday 43
  Firefly 22
  Jade 103
  Mai Tai 62
  Midnight's Kiss 112
  Mimosa 97
  Ocean Breeze 61
  The Blue Train 33

Daiquiri 56
Daisy 24
Death In The Afternoon 111
Diamond Fizz 91
Disco Dancer 90
Drambuie, Toffee Split 153
Dubonnet
  BVD 130
  Wedding Belle 27
Duke 94

El Diablo 124
El Toro 124

Faux Kir Royale 162
Firefly 22
Firelighter 148
First Night 83
Flirtini 105
Flying Grasshopper 46
Flying Scotsman 76
French Kiss 133
Frozen Peach Daiquiri 66
Fruit Cooler 167
Fuzzy Navel 38

Galliano
  A Sloe Kiss 21
  Harvey Wallbanger 40
  Josiah's Bay Float 136
gin
  A Sloe Kiss 21
  Alabama Slammer 152

Alaska 26
Bachelor's Bait 35
Belle Collins 19
Bleu Bleu Bleu 31
Bloodhound 25
Blue Blooded 30
Bride's Mother 27
Creole Lady 35
Daisy 24
Diamond Fizz 91
Firefly 22
Gin Rickey 20
Gin Sling 23
Grand Royal Clover
  Club 32
Green Lady 34
Hawaiian Orange
  Blossom 26
Kismet 95
London French 75 95
Long Island Iced Tea 45
Maiden's Prayer 23
Martini 18
Monte Carlo 104
Moonlight 28
Palm Beach 22
Pussycat 31
Sabrina 107
Saketini 34
Sloe Screw 131
Seventh Heaven 29
Singapore Sling 18
Teardrop 30
The Blue Train 33
Tom Collins 19
Wedding Belle 27
Ginger Fizz 174
Goddaughter 85
Grand Royal Clover Club 32
Green Lady 34

Harvey Wallbanger 40
Hawaiian Orange
  Blossom 26
Heavenly 84
Heavenly Days 120
High Voltage 125
Highland Fling 69
Hot Brandy Chocolate 87
Hurricane 57

Irish Coffee 155
Irish cream liqueur
  After Five 135
  B-52 142
  Banana Slip 129
  Bloody Brain 129
  Climax 145
  Irish Stinger 150
  Moo Moo 144
  Mudslide 149
  Rattlesnake 134
  Tricolour 143
Irish Mist
  Colleen 77
  Raspberry Mist 99

Jade 103
Jealousy 128
Josiah's Bay Float 136

Kahlúa
  After Five 135
  Mudslide 149
  Rattlesnake 134
  Voodoo 153
Kamikaze 39
Kir Lethale 109
Kir Royale 90
kirsch
  Cherry Kitsch 84
  Moonlight 28
Kismet 95

Klondike Cooler 72
Knicks Victory Cooler 166

Last Mango in Paris 47
London French 75 95
Long Boat 175
Long Island Iced Tea 45

Mai Tai 62
Maidenly Mimosa 159
Maiden's Prayer 23
Malibu
  Banana Colada 56
  Voodoo 153
Mango Lassi 168
Manhattan 73
maraschino
  Duke 94
  Peacemaker 106
  Queen of Memphis 133
  Seventh Heaven 29
  Tricolour 143
Marilyn Monroe 115
Martini 18
Mellow Mule 137
Metropolitan 52
Miami Beach 70
Midnight Cowboy 79
Midnight's Kiss 112
Midori
  Jade 103
  Queen of Memphis 133
Mimi 48
Mimosa 97
Mini Colada 158
Minted Diamonds 136
Mocha Cream 183
Mocha Slush 183
Monte Carlo 104
Moo Moo 144
Moonlight 28
Moscow Mule 51
Mudslide 149

Napoleon's Nightcap 154
New England Party 166
Night & Day 115
Non-Alcoholic Pimm's 187

Ocean Breeze 61
Old-Fashioned 73

Palm Beach 22
Peacemaker 106
Peach Floyd 145
Peachy Cream 173
Pear & Raspberry
  Delight 177
Peartini 41
Perky Pineapple 182
Piña Colada 58
Pink Heather 75
Pink Sherbet Royale 108
Pink Squirrel 147
Pink Whiskers 82
Plantation Punch 60
Pom Pom 182
port
  Plantation Punch 60
  Whiskey Sangaree 74
Pretty In Pink 113
Prohibition Punch 160
Pussycat 31

Queen of Memphis 133

Ranch Girl 162
Raspberry Lemonade 118
Raspberry Mist 99
Rattlesnake 134
Red Apple Sunset 161

red wine: Sangria 146
rosé wine: Summer
  Punch 121
Royal Julep 102
Royal Silver 114
rum
  Apple Breeze 118
  Bajan Sun 60
  Banana Colada 56
  Banana Daiquiri 137
  Blue Hawaiian 61
  Caribbean
    Champagne 102
  Club Mojito 59
  Cuba Libre 64
  Cuban 80
  Cuban Special 64
  Daiquiri 56
  Disco Dancer 90
  Frozen Peach Daiquiri 66
  Hurricane 57
  Josiah's Bay Float 136
  Long Island Iced Tea 45
  Mai Tai 62
  Mellow Mule 137
  Ocean Breeze 61
  Palm Beach 22
  Piña Colada 58
  Plantation Punch 60
  Rum Cobbler 65
  Rum Cooler 67
  Rum Noggin 65
  Sparkling Gold 98
  Spotted Bikini 42
  Strawberry Colada 57
  Zombie 63

Sabrina 107
St. Clements 178
Saketini 34
Salty Dog 39
Salty Puppy 185
sambuca
  Black Beauty 42
  Tornado 141
  Zander 132
San Joaquin Punch 114
San Remo 98
Sangria 146
Sangria Seca 165
schnapps
  After Five 135
  Bloody Brain 129
  Fuzzy Navel 38
  High Voltage 125
  Minted Diamonds 136
  Peach Floyd 145
  Sex On The Beach 38
  The Bentley 99
  Tornado 141
  Voodoo 153
  White Diamond
    Frappé 141
  Woo-Woo 37
Screwdriver 51
Sloe Screw 131
Sea Breeze 50
Seelbach 110
Seventh Heaven 29
Sex On The Beach 38
Shady Lady 144
Shamrock 72
Shirley Temple 158
Sidecar 81
Silk Stockings 125
Singapore Sling 18
Slush Puppy 171
Sober Sunday 174
Soft Sangria 180
Southern Champagne 106
Southern Comfort
  A Sloe Kiss 21
  Alabama Slammer 152

Plantation Punch 60
Southern Champagne 106
Sparkling Gold 98
Spotted Bikini 42
Strawberry Colada 57, 178
Summer Punch 121
Sunny Bay 49
Sunrise 181

Teardrop 30
tequila
  Bleu Bleu Bleu 31
  El Diablo 124
  El Toro 124
  Firefly 22
  High Voltage 125
  Long Island Iced Tea 45
  Shady Lady 144
  Silk Stockings 125
  Tequila Slammer 126
  Tequila Sunrise 127
Thai Fruit Cocktail 171
The Bentley 99
The Blue Train 33
The Gunner 176
The Queen's Cousin 111
The Reviver 78
The Stone Fence 116
Thistle 77
Thunderbird 47
Toffee Split 153
Tom Collins 19
Tornado 141
Tricolour 143
Triple Sec
  Banana Daiquiri 137
  Colleen 77
  Cosmopolitan 36
  Cuban Special 64
  Duke 94
  Hawaiian Orange
    Blossom 26
  Kamikaze 39
  Maiden's Prayer 23
  Royal Silver 114
  San Remo 98
  Seelbach 110
  Sidecar 81
  The Blue Train 33
  The Queen's Cousin 111
  Zombie 63

Under The Boardwalk 103

vermouth
  Amarettine 107
  Beadlestone 76
  Bloodhound 25
  Broken Negroni 110
  BVD 130
  Flying Scotsman 76
  Highland Fling 69
  Manhattan 73
  Martini 18
  Miami Beach 70
  Pink Whiskers 82
  Shamrock 72
  Thistle 77
Virgin Mary 164
vodka
  A Sloe Kiss 21
  Black Beauty 42
  Black Russian 128
  Bleu Bleu Bleu 31
  Bloody Caesar 44
  Bloody Mary 44
  Blue Lagoon 140
  Blue Monday 43
  Chocolate Martini 152
  Cordless Screwdriver 43
  Cosmopolitan 36
  Cranberry Collins 50
  Flirtini 105

Flying Grasshopper 46
Fuzzy Navel 38
Harvey Wallbanger 40
Kamikaze 39
Kir Lethale 109
Last Mango in Paris 47
Long Island Iced Tea 45
Metropolitan 52
Midnight's Kiss 112
Mimi 48
Moscow Mule 51
Mudslide 149
Peach Floyd 145
Peartini 41
Salty Dog 39
Screwdriver 51
Sea Breeze 50
Sex On The Beach 38
Spotted Bikini 42
Sunny Bay 49
The Queen's Cousin 111
Thunderbird 47
Vodka Espresso 53
Woo-Woo 37
Voodoo 153

Wedding Belle 27
whiskey/whisky
  Beadlestone 76
  Boston Sour 71
  Bourbon Milk Punch 139
  Champagne Sidecar 91
  Colleen 77
  Flying Scotsman 76
  French Kiss 133
  Highland Fling 69
  Irish Coffee 155
  Klondike Cooler 72
  Manhattan 73
  Miami Beach 70
  Old-Fashioned 73
  Pink Heather 75
  Queen of Memphis 133
  Royal Julep 102
  Seelbach 110
  Shamrock 72
  The Stone Fence 116
  Thistle 77
  Whiskey Rickey 68
  Whiskey Sangaree 74
  Whiskey Sling 69
  Whiskey Sour 68
White Cosmopolitan 151
White Diamond Frappé 141
white wine
  Kamikaze 39
  Moonlight 28
white wine, sparkling
  Amarettine 107
  Black Velvet 101
  Broken Negroni 110
  Death In The... 111
  Disco Dancer 90
  Duke 94
  Kir Lethale 109
  Marilyn Monroe 115
  Midnight's Kiss 112
  Monte Carlo 104
  Night & Day 115
  Pink Heather 75
  Pink Sherbet Royale 108
  Pretty In Pink 113
  Raspberry Mist 99
  Royal Silver 114
  San Joaquin Punch 114
  Seelbach 110
  Tequila Slammer 126
  The Queen's Cousin 111
Wild Silk 100
Woo-Woo 37

Zander 132
Zombie 63